IRELAND

IRELAND

Sarah Elliott

RYDON
PUBLISHING

A Rydon Publishing Book
35 The Quadrant
Hassocks
West Sussex
BN6 8BP
www.rydonpublishing.co.uk
www.rydonpublishing.com

First published by Rydon Publishing in 2017

A CIP catalogue record for this book is available from the British Library.

ISBN: 978-1-910821-13-8

Printed in Poland by BZ Graf

CONTENTS

INTRODUCTION

Often referred to as the 'Emerald Isle', Ireland is known the world over for its beautiful scenery. At the very edge of Western Europe cradled by the Irish Sea and the Atlantic Ocean this beautiful country is alive with history. The vibrant countryside and rolling hills are dotted with the ruins of castles and monasteries that hint at stories of ancient ancestors. These relics of the past link the Stone Age with Saint Patrick and the Vikings with the Normans. They bring to life the history of an island nation that was plundered by many but fought hard to preserve its unique identity. Ireland's early history is abundant with folklore, legend and spirituality from the story of how the majestic Giant's Causeway got its name to the reasons behind the unique positioning of Newgrange, a passage tomb in the Boyne Valley. This intriguing stone structure is older than both Stonehenge in England and the pyramids of Egypt in Giza!

Ireland's unique position on the very west of Europe meant it was all but ignored by the Romans. Centuries later the Vikings in their longships battled against the treacherous Irish weather, pillaging remote Irish monasteries and coming ashore and founding what are now some of Ireland's oldest cities. Their predecessors, the Normans were responsible for many of the castles that can be explored throughout the country. From the plantations to the revolutionary years the effect of the British Empire's hold on Ireland shaped the island's history. The Great

Giant's Causeway

Round tower, Ireland

Famine saw the population of the island nation decimated. Many emigrated creating a link with the United States of America that still exists today. Throughout these tumultuous years the Irish fought hard to maintain their culture and later to revive the Gaelic language and embrace the legends and folklores of earlier centuries. Story-telling had always been a part of Irish culture and for the size and population of Ireland, the contribution its poets, playwrights and novelists have given to generations of readers and scholars is immense. From Oscar Wilde to WB Yeats, Edna O'Brien and Seamus Heaney the Irish have given the world a wealth of wonderful wordsmiths!

Ireland's history is so rich and diverse it throws up lots of amazing facts to discover; which revolutionary leader thought it sensible to show his prize Kerry Blue dog during an after-dark curfew? Where is Ireland's answer to the Taj Mahal? What is the world's longest running chat show? Who was the first woman to be elected to the House of Commons? These questions are answered and many more amazing and extraordinary facts revealed inside the pages of this book.

Sarah Elliot
Dublin, 2017

The Emerald Isle
Why Ireland has forty shades of green

Perched on the northwest tip of Europe, Ireland is a country that is known the world over for its luscious green landscape. By the time our earliest ancestors arrived in Ireland approximately 9,000 years ago, Ireland was blanketed in trees. As Ireland moved from the Mesolithic to the Neolithic periods some of the woods and forests were cleared. As the centuries progressed this continued, leaving the cities such as Dublin, Cork and Belfast as urban centres and the more rural countryside predominantly green. The Irish weather has a big part to play in maintaining the country's moniker home to forty shades of green. It is not just a question of latitude; many other places, such as Newfoundland, sit roughly the same distance north of the equator as Ireland but they are not nearly as green. It is Ireland's position in the middle of the Gulf Stream that dictates its weather and as a result, how plants and vegetation grow. It is why temperatures in Ireland

are pretty stable, neither getting too much sunshine in summer or snowfall in winter. Average rainfall varies from coast to coast. On the east coast the average number of rainy days is approximately 150 a year. The west coast gets more, with some parts having rain around 225 days a year. The longest ever period of time without rain in Ireland was in Limerick in 1938 when there was no rain between 3 April and 10 May. But without the rain there would be no emerald isle. The first time the words '*Emerald Isle*' ever appeared in print in reference to Ireland was in a poem by William Drennan from Belfast titled '*When Erin First Rose*'. And so this romantic epithet we have come to associate with Ireland, was born.

Alas! for poor Erin that some are
*   still seen,*
Who would dye the grass red from
*   their hatred to green;*
Yet, oh! when you're up, and
*   they're down, let them live,*
Then yield them that mercy which
*   they would not give.*
Arm of Erin, be strong! but be

*   gentle as brave;*
And uplifted to strike, be still
*   ready to save;*
Let no feeling of vengeance
*   presume to defile*
The cause of, or men of, the
*   Emerald Isle.*

Giant steps and baby steps
The Giant's Causeway

On the North coast of Ireland reaching out into the Atlantic Ocean is one of the most spectacular UNESCO word Heritage Sites. Formed from basalt rock almost 60 million years ago, a pathway of some 40,000 symmetrical columns descends from the North Antrim cliffs into the ocean below. This dramatic site has inspired tales of ancient Irish giants who used the basalt pavement to stride across to Scotland. The legend tells of the Irish giant Finn McCool, (an anglicized and enlarged version of the warrior Fionn Mac Cumháil) who features heavily in Irish mythology. Benandonner, a Scottish giant was Finn's greatest rival. They roared at each other across the sea but had never met. Finn decided that it was time to go into battle once and for all. He tore chunks off the Antrim coast and flung them into the sea, forming a pathway for his rival to cross. On seeing the size of Benandonner, Finn ran back to his home where his quick-thinking wife Oonagh dressed him up like a baby in a makeshift crib. She invited Finn's nemesis in for tea and when Benandonner clapped eyes on the size of Finn's baby he shot back across the causeway to Scotland, never to be seen on Irish shores again.

Despite this popular legend the path-like structure does not actually continue underwater towards the Scottish coast. It ends quite abruptly giving way to a seabed of sand and shell. Scientists have been fascinated with the unusual honeycomb structure of the rocks for over 300 years. Their studies reveal that the Giant's Causeway was formed as a result of volcanic activity beneath the sea. Boiling lava rose up from the earth's crust. On contact with

the surface the lava immediately cooled. While the temperature fell the lava dried out, and it was this drying that caused the solidifying lava to crack and form regular pillars of basalt rock. The size and shape of each basalt column was determined by the rate at which the lava cooled and dried; the slower the cooling the larger the basalt columns. This also caused a variation in the number of sides on each column. There are columns with four, five, six, seven, eight and nine sides. Only one column has just three sides. The end result is this amazing honeycomb-like structure

The Giant's Causeway

that extends from the coast into the sea. The result is so dramatic that when the site was first studied in the 17th century it was believed to be a manmade structure formed using picks and chisels rather than a naturally formed geometric pattern.

Older than the pyramids!
The New Stone Age / Neolithic period

Around 4,000 BC Neolithic people began to populate Ireland, clearing the dense forests with stone axes to create large, localized communities. They built rectangular dwellings separated into rooms, not dissimilar from modern houses. They fashioned bowls and pots from wood and clay that was hardened over fires and used for cooking. Preserved examples of these early civilisations can be seen at the Céide Fields in County Mayo. This site shows the extent to which these New Stone Age people had moved on from the more nomadic existence of the Mesolithic period (8,000 BC–4,000

BC). Over a period of about 500 years they cleared over 1,000 acres of woodland and developed a complex enclosed field system suitable for farming. They grew cereal crops and tended cattle, sheep and goats.

A series of large Megalithic tombs can also be found at the Céide fields. These are evidence that the New Stone Age people believed in an afterlife. While they were used as burial places or places of worship it is also believed that these impressive stone structures were used to delineate territory and can be found dotted across the Irish landscape.

Court tombs, portal tombs and passage tombs are the three main types of tomb found in Ireland. Court tombs consist of a series of large stones shaped in a semi-circle leading to a rectangular or wedge-shaped tomb. An example of such a tomb can be found at Creevykeel, County Sligo. Portal tombs are probably the most recognisable of all the tombs. Also known as dolmens they consist of three or more upright stones, topped by a massive downward sloping capstone.

The dolmen at Poulnabrone, County Clare is the oldest dated Megalithic monument in Ireland. Archaeological excavations revealed the remains of twenty-one people in its main passageway. Radiocarbon dating of their bones proved that the tomb was used as a burial place over a period of 600 years between 3,800 BC and 3,200 BC. Further analysis of these skeletons revealed that they died at a young age with only one skeleton aged over forty. The bones show evidence of arthritis – indicative of manual labour and carrying heavy loads. Construction of such tombs may have played a part in this. It is not known how these tombs were made. The weight of the stones and boulders used must have required a system of ropes, wooden planks, and harnessed the power of animals.

The most well known example of Irish Neolithic construction is Newgrange, a passage tomb in the Boyne Valley in County Meath. Built around 3,200 BC this phenomenal structure is older than both Stonehenge in England and the pyramids of Giza in Egypt. Newgrange is a large circular

Newgrange

mound, 85 metres (278 feet) in diameter and 13.5 metres (44 feet) high. The mound is surrounded by 97 kerbstones, some of which are engraved with Megalithic carvings. Inside is a 19 metre (62 feet) stone passageway, chambers and a roof-light. It is here that Newgrange reveals itself to be more than your average Megalithic tomb. Every year on the winter solstice as the sun rises over Newgrange the beam of light it radiates travels through the roof-box illuminating the chamber within for 17 minutes. Every year people gather at the site of Newgrange to celebrate the winter solstice. The visitor centre holds an annual lottery for tickets as only a limited number of people can actually enter the passage tomb and witness what our ancestors created almost 5,0000 years ago. Newgrange is part of a wider series of monuments known as *Brú na Boinne* which includes Knowth and Dowth. Why these amazing structures were built is still not fully understood but they represent human ingenuity and the human desire to connect with the natural world.

Veni, vidi, vici! Or maybe not...
Ireland and the Roman Empire

Veni, vidi, vici announced Caesar but whether this cry was ever uttered in relation to Ireland is debatable. The discovery of sites of archaeological importance, particularly at Faughan Hill in County Meath and Drumanagh, near Skerries in County Dublin, reignited the debate on whether there was a Roman invasion in Ireland. Examination of the available evidence indicates that this was unlikely but that there was contact of some kind. Rather than being evidence of a Roman invasion, the artefacts that were discovered are more than likely evidence of travel and trading between Ireland and other European countries.

The fact that the Romans referred to Ireland as Hiberna meaning '*land of winter*' indicates that they were aware of it and its changeable climate. Caesar was the first Roman writer to refer to it, correctly assuming that it was smaller than Britain. A 2nd century Greek

Roman soldiers

geographer named Claudius Ptolemy used Roman military charts to construct an outline map of the British Isles, including Ireland. Ptolemy's map positions Ireland surprisingly accurately and he did get the name of some of the major rivers correct. Some of the place names however continue to cause confusion. The accuracy in positioning Ireland points

towards travellers from other countries visiting Ireland by boat.

One of the problems that the Romans experienced in securing western Britain was that Britain's sea frontier included hundreds of miles of rugged coastline stretching from Cornwall in the south to Scotland in the north. As long as Ireland remained unconquered, renegades from Britain could always escape to Ireland. The Irish Sea was recognized as an important conduit for the movement of people and goods and therefore invading and securing Ireland would provide greater security for the Roman Empire as a whole. Despite that, it never happened and Ireland remained an independent haven on the edge of Europe until the British Empire spread westwards.

Natural preservatives
Ireland's Bog men

In the centre of Ireland rising from the Bog of Allen is the remains of what was once a volcano. Known as Croghan Hill, the 232 metre (761 foot) mound provides extensive views of the predominantly flat bogland surroundings. The area gives its name to the preserved remains of a body that was found beneath the bog by peat workers in 2003. Fifteen miles (25 kilometres) away another male body was discovered when a peat-cutting machine severed a preserved torso in half. Radiocarbon dating showed that Old Croghan Man lived between 362 and 175 BC and Clonycavan Man lived between 392 and 201 BC. Both men appeared to have had violent deaths with signs of trauma found on their skeletons. Although Old Croghan Man is missing his head and lower limbs, a team of archaeologists estimated his height at an impressive 198cm (six feet six inches). His fingertips and hands show signs of a man that did not have to carry out manual labour. It is known that his last meal consisted of buttermilk and cereals although the condition of his nails revealed that his normal diet was rich in meat. The neighbouring Clonycavan man was a lot smaller in stature measuring just 157cm (five feet two inches). Further inspection of his remains revealed that he used an early form of hair gel! The 'gel' was made of a mixture of vegetable plant oil mixed with resin from pine trees found in Spain and southwest France.

Such findings provide intriguing insights into the lives of those that came before us. The peaty wetlands offer cold, acidic, oxygen-free conditions, which are perfect for preventing decay and mummifying human flesh. In Ireland these areas are referred to as bogs, derived from the Gaelic word *bogarch,* meaning soft. Ireland has the third highest proportion of peatland in the world after Canada and Finland. It is predominantly found in the midlands and the Bog of Allen is the largest bog in Ireland.

Land of the little people
The myth of the leprechaun

Although it is one of Ireland's most enduring myths unfortunately the sloping hills of Ireland are not awash with tiny creatures sporting green waistcoats and shiny shoes. The myth of the leprechaun has its origins in Irish folk and fairy lore. It is thought that the name comes from the ancient Irish word *luchorpán* meaning little man or *luacharmán* meaning pygmy. That phrase has been used in texts dating from the 8th century in reference to a community of little people with magical powers. Their stories are similar to those of other diminutive fairy figures such as sprites, gnomes and pixies. Some earlier texts refer to these little guys wearing red clothing but green is now the colour most associated with this cheeky Irish imp.

Most myths and tales concerning the leprechaun indicate a devious character. The leprechaun is always male and his profession is a cobbler or shoe-maker. Legend suggests that the leprechaun has hidden a pot of gold at the end of the rainbow. Most of the tales regarding the leprechaun are actually fables pertaining to being happy with your lot and to stop searching for the metaphoric pot of gold. Quite deep for a hammer-wielding little guy with a red beard and green waistcoat!

BOO!

Halloween has its origins in Irish mythology. The celebration was originally conceived by the Celts who settled in Ireland from Europe, including parts of France, Spain, Scotland and Wales. They were great story-tellers and believed in the legend of the **Tuath de Danann,** *Irish gods and goddesses that were forced underground to live as fairy folk following their defeat by the Milesians.*

In Celtic Ireland about 2,000 years ago, Samhain was the division of the year, a brief window between summer and winter. At Samhain the division between the earthly world and the spiritual world was at its finest allowing spirits to pass through from the spiritual realm to the earthly world. People wore masks and costumes to ward off any roaming ghosts. Bonfires were lit and feasts prepared for both the living and the dead. It was the equivalent celebration of modern New Year's Eve and signified the end of one season and the beginning of the next.

Here, boy!
The Irish wolfhound

> *Eyes of sloe, with ears not low,*
> *A horse's breast, with depth of chest*
> *A breadth of loin, with curve of groin,*
> *And nape set far behind the head,*
> *Such were the dogs that Fingal bred.*

This is a 5th century description of an Irish wolfhound from the writings of Oisín, son of Fionn Mac Cumhaill. This giant of a dog is synonymous with Irish legends, in particular the story of how Ireland's most famous mythological hero, Cúchulainn, got his name. According to the legend, Cúchulainn (or Setanta as he was called at the time) killed the hound using his hurl and sliotar after the horse-sized animal charged at him. He was guarding the home of his Uncle Culann. Setanta was distraught at having killed the giant dog and offered to take his place as his uncle's guard, hence the name Cúchulainn meaning the 'Hound of Culann'.

But this is not the earliest mention of the Irish wolfhound. The breed was well known in Roman days. The first authentic reference was recorded in 391 AD when the Roman Consul, Quintus Aurelius Symmachus, thanks Flavianus, for a gift of Irish dogs. The dog's size, agility and hunting prowess meant that it was much sought after throughout Europe. The Irish wolfhound was originally bred to hunt wolves so it had to be fast enough to overtake a wolf and powerful enough to kill it. By the end of the 18th century Irish wolves had been hunted to extinction. With the demise of this wild animal came the demise of the Irish wolfhound.

An English army captain, George A. Graham (1833–1909) had always been fascinated with this majestic breed and took it upon himself to bring the breed back from the edge of extinction. He managed to bring a number of dogs from Ireland to his estate in Gloucestershire, England. It is believed that the Irish wolfhounds were not the same breed that had travelled to Rome or fought with the Fianna. Throughout the years they bred with other dogs and Graham continued crossing the Irish wolfhounds with Borzois, Great Danes, Deerhounds and Mastiffs. He founded the Irish Wolfhound Club in 1885 and the dog so synonymous with Celtic legends became popular once again. When the Free State introduced its first coinage in 1928 featuring a series of domestic and wild animals, the Irish wolfhound appeared on the sixpence until decimalization was introduced in 1971.

Irish wolfhound

CONVICT 224

Ireland does not have a national dog but if Michael Collins (1890–1922) had his way it would be the Kerry Blue Terrier. Shortly before his assassination Collins had proposed that the Kerry Blue Terrier be officially recognized as the dog of the Irish Free State. Collins was enamoured with the breed so much so that he risked his life to show his dog, Convict 224, at a breed show in Dublin on 16 October 1920. Also at the dog show was British Captain, Wyndham Quinn, who resided at the Vice Regal Lodge in the Pheonix Park. He presented the winning trophy which bore his name. The Under Secretary for Ireland, Sir James McMahon, also competed alongside the most wanted man in Ireland. At this time Collins had a £10,000 price on his head and he was one of the reasons that a nightly curfew was in place on the streets of Dublin. The names of other dogs on show that night are indicative of the charged political landscape. Munster Fusilier,

Kerry Blue Terrier

Markavich [sic], Trotsky, and Dawn of Freedom lined up alongside Collins's Convict 224.

Today, under the auspices of the Irish Kennel Club, the 'Collins Cup' is annually awarded to best of breed at the Kerry Blue Terrier show.

May the blessings of Saint Patrick behold you
The spread of Christianity in Ireland

Saint Patrick is possibly Ireland's most famous man but he did not actually come from Ireland. It is believed that he came from Bannaventum Taburniae, a Romanized town in what is now thought to be Scotland or Wales. The *Confessio*, Patrick's short record of his life and one of the oldest documents in Irish history, provides an overview of his life and how he came to Ireland.

Taken by Irish pirates at the age of sixteen, Patrick was sold into slavery in Ireland. For six years he tended sheep on a mountain in an area believed to be County Mayo. The loneliness and remoteness of this existence contributed to Patrick's growing faith. In the *Confessio*, Patrick explains that he heard a voice, which he attributed to God, urging him to return to his family. He managed to escape, board a ship and return home. Once Patrick was reunited with his family, he embraced Christianity and became a priest. Once again, he dreamt that God had spoken to him, urging him to return to Ireland to spread Christianity.

Although the Roman Empire did not expand to Ireland, its vicinity to Britain meant that it did not remain outside its influence. Christianity had begun to appear in Ireland prior to Patrick's missionary efforts. In 431 AD, Pope Celestine sent a bishop, Palladius, to Ireland. However, it was the zealousness of Patrick and his dedicated followers in establishing churches, monasteries and schools around Ireland that led to Patrick becoming Primate of all Ireland and the reason why he is credited as the founder of Christianity in Ireland. Patrick began his mission to Ireland in 432 AD, and by his death in 461 AD, the island was almost entirely Christian.

Saint Patrick is one of Ireland's three patron saints and is recognized with a national holiday on 17 March. This is believed to be the date of his death. Parades are held throughout the world with many famous landmarks 'going green' including the Disney Castle in Shanghai, the Coliseum in Rome, Christ the Redeemer in Rio de Janeiro and Trinity College in Dublin. In fact the first ever Saint Patrick's Day parade was held in New York City in 1762 and still takes place today.

This status brings with it many myths; Patrick is credited with banishing snakes from Ireland but following the Ice Age there were probably not actually any snakes in Ireland to banish! The shamrock is also closely associated with the Saint, believing that he used the three-leafed clover to indicate the Father, the Son and the Holy Spirit. There is no proof of this yet every year the Irish don shamrocks on Saint Patrick's Day. A bowl of shamrock has been presented to the American president since 1952 when Irish ambassador to Washington John Hearne sent a box of it to President Harry S. Truman (1884–1972).

THE HOLY TRINITY

Ireland has three patron saints: Saint Patrick, Saint Brigid and Saint Columcille. St Columcille was born in County Donegal in the 5th century and was descended from great Irish nobility, tracing his ancestry to Niall of the Nine Hostages, the legendary Irish High King. He founded the monastery on the island of Iona off the coast of Scotland where it is believed that the **Book of Kells** *was produced. He is also known as Saint Columba and his feast day is 9 June.*

Saint Brigid was the daughter of a pagan King of Leinster and a Christian Pictish slave who had been baptised by St Patrick.

St Brigid's Cross

According to legend, St Brigid prayed that her beauty be taken away so that she could not marry and she became a nun. St Brigid famously converted a dying man by fashioning a cross from rushes she found on the ground which she used to bless him. She is believed to have been the first and only female bishop. Her feast day is celebrated on 1 February and in Catholic schools children create St Brigid's crosses to mark the day.

All three saints are interred in Downpatrick, County Down.

A medieval treasure
The Book of Kells

Housed in the 18th century Old Library at Trinity College, Dublin is one of the most important and prolific examples of medieval illumination and calligraphy in the world. Although the *Book of Kells* has been the result of in-depth study by scholars around the world, remarkably little is known about those who created it, or why this extraordinary manuscript was created. The *Book of Kells* consists of 680 pages, made up of 340 calf-skin leaves or vellum, written and decorated on each side. About 150 calves would have been required to produce this quantity of quality vellum. The book depicts the four Christian gospels. The title page of each gospel is the most ornate and extravagantly designed in the book.

To create the words and pictures the scribe would have fashioned a quill from goose feathers. A range of pigments were required to create the depth of colour on the highly decorated vellum pages. These were made from the juices of plants, leaves and other natural resources that were available to the monks. Blue was made from woad extracted from the leaves of the woad plant after they had been dried, powdered, and fermented. Orpiment was ground down to produce a vibrant gold pigment. Red was derived from red lead.

In-depth examination of the manuscript has revealed subtle variations in lettering, implying that it was possibly the work of at least four different scribe-artists.

Despite its name it is generally accepted that work on the book began in the monastery of Iona, an island off the Scottish coast, between 740 AD and 802 AD. Some scholars believe that it may have been commissioned in 797 AD to mark the 200 year

anniversary of St Columba who founded the monastery on Iona. After this period Iona was under attack on several occasions from Viking raiders. The level of detail and intricacy on the pages of the book would have been difficult to achieve at a time when the monastery was under threat. There are unfinished folios within the manuscript lending credence to the belief that the monks had to flee Iona leaving the manuscript unfinished. The abbot of Iona formed a new monastery at Kells. Medieval sources record that an illuminated manuscript was stolen from the stone church of Kells in 1006 which is likely to have been the *Book of Kells*. According to the *Annals of Ulster* the book was found '*two months and twenty days later*', '*under a sod*'. After that it is thought that the book was kept in the parish church in Kells until the arrival of Oliver Cromwell's army in 1654. The book was sent to Dublin by the governor of Kells for safekeeping. A few years later it reached Trinity College where it remains today. It is a myth that each day a different page of the book is turned, but the library always has one of the exquisite opening pages on display revealing the uniqueness of this fragile manuscript to the many visitors to the Trinity College library.

A long time ago, on an island far, far away...
The Skelligs

Eight miles (12 km) from the coast of Kerry, rising majestically from the sea are the rocky, uninhabited Skellig Islands. There are two islands: Skellig Michael and Small Skellig. They are formed from the same 350 million year old Devonian sandstone that can be found throughout the Kerry landscape. The largest of the Skelligs is Skellig Michael. Small Skellig is the second largest gannet colony in the world with 70,000 gannets nesting there annually. The very remote nature of these islands provides a place where seabirds can nest and rear their young.

Slightly more accessible, the rocky outpost of Skellig Michael on the edge of the southwest coast of Ireland was home to one of the earliest monastic settlements in the country. 217 metres (714 feet) above sea level and carved solely from stone is a remarkably well-preserved monastery. It is testament to the work of the 6th century monks who inhabited the island. It is believed that the monastery was founded by St Fionan. Under his guidance the monks chiselled a stairway from the stone leading to the top of Skellig Michael. From the landing site, it is a steep 670 step climb to the monastic site where the monks built six corbelled, beehive-shaped huts, two boat-shaped oratories, stone crosses, two wells and a church. The cells date from more than one period and reflect the development of drystone construction during the early medieval period. They are built so that they are round on the outside and rectangular on the inside and completely watertight. Like other monasteries throughout Europe the Skelligs were plundered throughout the 9th century by Viking attackers.

The Skellig Islands

There is little known about the years preceding the Vikings' reign of terror but the monastery was eventually abandoned in the 12th century. Skellig Michael remained a place of pilgrimage for hundreds of years afterward. Now it is a place of worship for a very different type of pilgrim; the majestic Skellig Islands feature prominently in the JJ Abrams's *Star Wars* movies and fans are flocking to visit the awe-inspiring location.

Battle of the boozers
The oldest pub in Ireland

The Irish pub is more than just a place to have a drink. It is a place where friends and family come together to eat, celebrate, watch sports, play traditional music, dance and maybe have a pint or two. The pub has been a part of Irish culture for centuries but which establishment can claim to be the oldest in Ireland? This is a dispute that had been going on for many years with the owners of Sean's Bar in Athlone Co. Westmeath and The Brazen Head on Merchant's Quay both claiming the accolade. The owner of Sean's bar had evidence to suggest that there was in fact a retail premises at the location in the heart of Ireland's midlands as far back as 900 AD. When the pub was renovated during the 1970s, the walls were found to be made of wattle and daub, dating back to the ninth century. Part of the wall is now on display at the National Museum along with old coins from the same period which were found by the builders. The floor is now officially a protected structure. The claim has since been thoroughly researched by the *Guinness Book of Records* revealing Sean's Bar to be the oldest in Europe. Sean's had to see off the challenge from the oldest pub in Britain: the Bingley Arms in Bardsey, North Leeds to win the title. It is widely believed that Sean's is in fact the oldest pub in the world but investigations into this are ongoing. For now the framed certificate from the Guinness Book of Records has pride of place on the wall of the bar alongside photos of its famous patrons including Larry Hagman of *Dallas* fame and Maureen Potter, one of Ireland's best-loved entertainers.

The Brazen Head has had a history of interesting clientele and was frequented by many of Ireland's literary elite. James Joyce famously referenced it in his universally acclaimed novel *Ulysses*. Brendan Behan and Jonathan Swift are thought to have popped by the establishment too. Although it may have lost the battle for oldest pub in Ireland The Brazen Head can boast the oldest graffiti in Ireland. A signature etched on a window was confirmed to be from 1726. The etching is so small that a magnifying glass is required to read the inscription *'John Langan halted here 7 August 1726'*.

Leopold Bloom, the central character in James Joyce's afore-mentioned Ulysses, famously said that it would be a good puzzle to walk across Dublin without passing a pub. In 2011 computer programmer Rory McCann used an algorithm to take on the challenge. Despite Joyce setting the puzzle back in 1922 when there were more pubs in Dublin, it took McCann several weeks to solve. In 2014 he modified the route to exclude hotels. The route takes in St James' Gate, the home of Guinness, but as McCann pointed out, you cannot pay for a pint at the brewery. Fittingly the route includes a stroll across the James Joyce Bridge.

Urbs Intacta: the Untaken City
Ireland's oldest city

Founded by Viking raiders in 914 AD, Waterford is Ireland's oldest city. It is the largest settlement in Ireland to retain its original Norse or Viking derived place name, *Vaderfiord* meaning 'haven from the wind-swept sea'. The trading importance of the Suir, Barrow and Nore rivers, known commonly as the *'three sisters,'* and their tributaries, cannot be underestimated in understanding the reason that the Vikings settled here. Having raided monasteries throughout Ireland in the 8th and 9th centuries they established a longphort or dock at the confluence of St John's River and the River Suir and the beginnings of a city emerged. Shortly after, they established their City-State appointing their own bishop. Waterford grew in wealth and prestige, and gradually the Viking raiders became entwined with the Gaelic Irish through alliances and even marriage.

In 1137 the settlement was surrounded by Diarmuid McMurrough, King of Leinster. Diarmuid was later banished from his kingdom by Roderick O'Conor, the High King of Ireland, for abducting the wife of O'Rorke, another chieftain. Diarmuid wanted his Kingdom back. He sought assistance from Henry II, King of England. Henry authorized Diarmuid to raise an army from among the Anglo-Normans in Wales. The first Anglo-Normans landed in Wexford in 1169 and began the process of helping Diarmuid win back his kingdom. A second invasion led by Strongbow sailed into passage East in Waterford. In order to win Strongbow's support Diarmuid had promised him the hand of his daughter Aoife if he captured Waterford and helped restore him to his rightful position as King of Leinster. A fierce and bloody battle ensued and Waterford fell to Strongbow on 25 August 1170. Later that day Strongbow and Aoife were married heralding the end of

Viking Longboat

the old order. The Normans continued their raid on Ireland. By 1250 two-thirds of the country was controlled by them. Although their introduction into Ireland was violent and bloody, the Anglo-Normans began the long and slow process towards democracy and parliamentary representation. A bronze statue of Strongbow and Aoife can be found at the Bishop's Palace Garden in the heart of the Viking Triangle in Waterford.

PAY THROUGH THE NOSE
It is believed that the origin of the phrase 'to pay through the nose' comes from the Vikings' penchant for slitting the nose from tip to eyebrow of anyone who refused to pay their taxes. This was referred to by the people of Waterford as Airgead Sróine or nose money.

From Castle to Kingdom
The evolution of a town

Trim Castle is one of the finest examples of a Norman castle in Ireland. Perched on a hill above the town the castle played an important role in protecting the town that grew up around it from attack. You may recognize the imposing structure – Trim Castle and the surrounding areas feature heavily in the Hollywood movie about Scotland's William Wallace Braveheart. Surrounded by rich, fertile land the area provided an ideal location for a medieval settlement. The high grounds on the outskirts of the town provided a means of defence while the River Boyne meant that Trim was accessible in terms of trading networks throughout Ireland and beyond. The proximity to trading links meant that Trim was able to grow into a bustling medieval town with weekly markets and annual fairs. Throughout the Middle Ages Trim was connected to the de Lacys; the de Genevilles; the

Trim Castle

Mortimers and Richard, Duke of York. Evidence of these connections can be seen throughout the town.

Sloping down from the castle gate, known as the town gate, is a winding path leading down to the town and what would have been a busy medieval market place. Now referred to as Market Street, what was once the market place in medieval times is evident. What remains is a short, broad street which widens towards the east end. This widening would have facilitated market stalls and livestock pens, leaving room for both buyers and sellers to congregate. In the 12th century permission had been granted to hold an annual fair at Trim, beginning on 21 February and lasting for eight days. By the 15th century this had become a summer fair. This was more in line with what happened throughout

Ireland. A fair was held once a year and a market was held weekly, usually on a Thursday.

Although little evidence of shops or taverns remains in Trim, street names indicate that such establishments did exist. Take Fishamble Street for example. This street name survived as a name up until the 18th century in Trim. Often fish markets were held away from the main market and the fact that such a street existed demonstrates that the medieval inhabitants of Trim bought and sold fish in this particular area, away from the main market. Likewise Cornmarket Street suggests an area where corn was sold. We know that wheat, oats and corn were important grain crops in Meath partly due to the fact that the River Boyne was used to harness power for milling. Wine Street and Wynetavern Street were names that survived after the middle ages too. Although no archaeological evidence of such establishments exist the street name indicates that there was a drinking culture in this particular area of the town.

WHAT'S IN A NAME?

Perhaps the most romantically named road in Ireland, Lovers Walk, is on the road from Montenotte to Tivoli in Cork City. Some believe that the road got its name because this is where famed nationalist and rebellion Robert Emmett (1778–1803) walked arm in arm with his lover Sara Curran before the failed uprising of 1803 and Emmet's subsequent execution. Local legend has it that Sara Curran continued to walk the road mourning the loss of her love. How the road actually got its name is a case of lost in translation rather than everlasting love. The name in Gaelic means the Walk of the

Leper in costume, with clapper and basket

Lepers. *There was a leprosarium outside Cork City, near Glanmire and pilgrims visiting the hospital would disembark from their ships on the River Lee then walk to the hospital using the road.*

In fact many Irish place names are anglicized versions of the original Gaelic place name. Anglo–Norman settlers began translating the names based on how they were pronounced rather than by direct translation. This was later continued by the British as they surveyed the land for tax purposes. As the example of Lovers Walk shows this often means it looks as if a particular place name means one thing when it actually means something completely different!

The Gift of the Gab
Kissing the Blarney Stone

Built nearly 600 years ago Blarney Castle is home to the famous Blarney Stone. Legend dictates that anyone who kisses it is bestowed with the gift of eloquence and the skill of flattery or, put simply, the gift of the gab! How it came to Blarney Castle is unclear resulting in mythological explanations that only add to the stones' mysterious appeal.

One legend tells of Cormac Laidir MacCarthy, Lord of Muskerry and the Irish goddess of love, Cliodhna. Cormac was apparently being brought to court and he was so worried he was going to lose that he prayed to Cliodhna asking for her help. Cliodhna told him to kiss the first stone that he came across on his way to court. He did as he was told and in court his new found gift of the gab ensured that he won his case. Legend has it that Cormac went back for the stone and brought it to Blarney Castle where it continues to work its magic today.

Another tale involves Queen

Elizabeth I

Elizabeth I and Cormac Teige McCarthy. Queen Elizabeth I demanded that Irish Chieftans surrendered the right to their castles and lands to the British Crown. The popular myth is that Cormac Teige MacCarthy kissed the Blarney Stone and charmed his way out of having to sign over Blarney Castle.

Another myth links the stone to Scotland. In 1314, Cormac McCarthy sent 5,000 men to aid Robert the Bruce and Scotland in their fight against the English at the Battle of Bannockburn. As a token of gratitude it is believed that Robert the Bruce gifted Cormac a piece of the Stone of Scone or the Stone of Destiny, a stone that for centuries was associated with the crowning of Scottish kings. The stone was then brought back to Blarney and set into the castle walls.

There are many other stories including that the stone was St Columba's deathbed pillow and some have even suggested that the Blarney Stone was struck by Moses in the desert creating a flow of water that quenched the thirst of his people. How the stone made its way to Blarney is another story altogether.

In 2014 geologists from Glasgow University examined a microscopic slide of the stone and revealed that the stone comes from local carboniferous limestone synonymous with Ireland. This would indicate that it has nothing to do with Stonehenge, the Stone of Scone or in fact Moses but that doesn't make for quite as good a story, does it?

THE KISS OF DEATH

The Blarney stone is built into the defensive parapet surrounding Blarney Castle. Kissing it is in actual fact quite a difficult feat. In

Blarney Castle

the past, in order to kiss the stone people were hung by their feet over the parapet. Nowadays it is not quite so dangerous. Iron bars have been erected to hold on to while you hang back and lock lips with the magic limestone.

Who run the world? Girls!

Ireland's Pirate Queen and England's Queen Elizabeth I

Referred to as Grace O'Malley (1530–1603) and Granuaile, Gráinne Ní Mháille is probably better known as Gráinne Mhaol or Ireland's Pirate Queen. Born into Irish aristocracy in 1530, her story centres around the 16th century Tudor conquest of Ireland under Queen Elizabeth I. Gráinne was an only child and under Brehon law when her Chieftan father died she inherited his territory. The O'Malleys controlled the coastline along the West of Ireland, patrolling them as pirates and demanding taxes from fishermen and traders.

This however was at a time when the British Crown was beginning to tighten its hold on Ireland. Throughout her life Gráinne Mhaol battled against the crown to hold onto her land and the land of her peers. When the English governor of Connaught, Sir Richard Bingham captured Gráinne's son Theobald, legend has it she set sail for England to speak directly to Queen Elizabeth. She sailed up the River Thames in London, and met Queen Elizabeth at Greenwich. The women were roughly the same age – one the Queen of England, the other the Queen of the Irish seas. Queen Elizabeth could not speak Irish and Gráinne Mhaol did not speak English so the two most powerful women in Britain and Ireland conversed in Latin. It is believed that Gráinne Mhaol impressed Queen Elizabeth as she subsequently granted the Pirate Queen her requests on condition that she cease all rebellious activity against the crown. This was short-lived however and although her son

The meeting of Gráinne Mhaol and Queen Elizabeth I

was released, the terms of the agreement made with the Monarch were later rebuked. Gráinne Mhaol died at Rockfleet Castle in 1603, the same year as Queen Elizabeth.

Ireland's most famous head-case
Oliver Plunkett

In St Peter's Church in the centre of Drogheda in County Louth rests the head and a selection of bones from the body of Oliver Plunkett (1625–1681). Born in Oldcastle in County Meath, Oliver Plunkett would go on to become a priest, spending a large part of his life studying and worshipping in Italy. Unable to return to Ireland which was under attack from Oliver Cromwell (1599–1658) and his army, Plunkett continued with his studies going on to become a professor of theology. Following Cromwell's death and the subsequent death of the Archbishop of Armagh it was deemed safe to allow Plunkett to return to Ireland as Archbishop.

Once on Irish soil he began

his work as Archbishop in earnest helping set up schools. However, once again anti-Catholic activity reared its head. On 4 October 1670, the Council of Ireland decreed that all bishops and priests must leave the country by 20 November. When the Earl of Essex was appointed Viceroy of Ireland in 1672, he banned Catholic education and exiled priests. Oliver Plunkett refused to leave. He travelled the country dressed as a layman, confirming people throughout the countryside. He was eventually arrested on 6 December 1679 and hanged for false charges of planning to bring 20,000 French soldiers to Ireland and planning an uprising. On 11 July 1681, Oliver Plunkett was executed in front of a crowd. He publicly announced his forgiveness of those who were responsible for his capture and death. He was beatified in 1920 and canonised in 1975, the first new Irish saint for almost seven hundred years.

Now his head rests in a cage on a church wall in Drogheda. His left clavicle, left scapula, ninth and

Oliver Plunkett

tenth rib, left hemi-pelvic bone and sacrum are also held at the church. Every year on the Sunday prior to his Feast Day there is a procession through the streets of Drogheda led by a bier carrying the Saint's bones.

Soldiers in petticoats
*The suffragette movement
in Ireland*

In July 1912 the English Prime Minister Herbert Henry Asquith (1852–1928) almost lost his head when an English suffragette hurled a hatchet at him during a visit to the Irish capital. John Redmond (1856–1918), leader of the Irish Parliamentary Party narrowly missed losing his shoulder. Although Asquith was a Liberal, his liberal policies did not include extending the right to vote to women. The women responsible for the militant action were Mary Leigh and Gladys Evans, members of the Women's Social and Political Union (WSPU). The society formed in London and led by Emmeline and Christabel Pankhurst had established branches in Belfast and Dublin. Their tactics were more violent than those employed by the Irish suffrage movement but some felt that this was necessary in order to progress achieving votes for women.

The suffrage movement in Ireland began in earnest in the 1860s when Isabella Todd (1836–1896) and Anna Haslam (1829–1922) led the Irish aspect of a campaign to change the law on women's property rights. Prior to this a single woman could own property but once she married, everything passed to her husband. The husband could even lay claim to any money his wife earned. Parliament passed acts throughout the 1870s and in 1882 which changed these restrictions on married women's

Herbert Henry Asquith

property. In 1876 Haslam and her husband founded a movement to extend these restrictions further by demanding votes for women. Both Todd and Haslam travelled extensively, speaking to their peers on the importance of extending the vote to include eligible women. Their campaigns were peaceful and centred around educating both men and women on the importance of equality and writing letters to parliament.

In 1908 Hanna Sheehy-Skeffington (1871–1946) and her husband Francis (1878–1916) helped to form a new suffrage group, the Irish Women's Franchise League (IWFL). This was in reaction to the lack of progress that the peaceful methods employed to date had elicited. Influenced by their peers in Britain the IWFL adopted more militant means of protest, organizing demonstrations and interrupting Redmond and other politicians at public meetings. They even brought the Pankhursts over to speak on a number of occasions. Between 1912 and 1914 thirty-five

Suffragettes, 1911

women including Hanna Sheehy-Skeffington were convicted of suffrage offences. This activity increased awareness of women's suffrage at a time when Irish politics was mainly concerned with Home Rule.

Mary Leigh and Gladys Evans were arrested and imprisoned for the attempted assassination of Prime Minister Asquith in 1912. They went on hunger strike and Irish suffragists such as Sheehy-Skeffington joined them. They were soon released from prison without being forcefed. Hanna Sheehy-Skeffington lost her job as a teacher as a result of her imprisonment. This level of militancy turned the Irish newspapers against the suffrage movement resulting in a change of public support so the groups began to dissociate themselves from the WSPU. When Britain went to war the suffrage movement was put on hold.

The outbreak of World War I and the contribution women played in society during these tumultuous years ensured that the government could no longer deny women the right to vote. In 1918 women over thirty years of age with a property qualification were granted suffrage. At ninety years of age Anna Haslam became one of the first Irish women to cast a vote.

WORKERS UNITE!
The first ever Irish Union for women was set up in Ireland by the sister of James 'Big Jim' Larkin in Dublin in the summer of 1911. Delia was born in Liverpool to Irish emigrants. James Larkin had left the Liverpool docks for Belfast in 1907 where he became a union organizer for dock labourers. Following a move to Dublin in a bid to organize workers in Dublin, Cork and Waterford Larkin founded the Irish Transport and General Workers Union (ITGWU). Delia followed her older brother from Liverpool to Dublin where she was tasked with organizing a union for female workers. The Irish Women Workers Union (IWWU) was formed and the job of recruiting members began. The union advertised for members in the **Irish**

Worker, *the weekly paper for the ITGWU set up by Jim Larkin. A month later the IWWU was launched. Its base was at Liberty Hall, Dublin. Numbers gradually increased and soon the union had over 1,000 affiliates. Jacob's Biscuit Factory had the largest number of members. During the 1913 lock-out over 300 female workers from Jacob's Factory were locked out of work for wearing the union badge in support of the striking tram workers. Following the lock-out trade union numbers dropped and Delia eventually returned to London where she helped with the war effort.*

When Delia Larkin died in 1949, she was buried beside her brother James and her brother Peter in Dublin's Glasnevin cemetery.

From Baltimore to Barbary
The Sack of Baltimore

In 1631 a crew of more than 200 Barbary pirates plundered the town of Baltimore in West Cork in a brutal night-time raid. It is believed that throughout the 300 years in which the Barbary Coast pirates were active they kidnapped over a million Europeans to sell at the massive slave market in Algiers. This was the first and only attempt at slave-raiding by the African pirates on the Irish coast.

Two ships left Algiers with a combined force of Dutch, Algerians and Turks under the command of one of the most successful leaders of Barbary pirates, a Dutch convert to Islam, Captain Morat Rais (c.1570–1641).

By 19 June the raiders were off the Old Head of Kinsale. Here they captured two fishing-boats from Dungarvan. One was captained by John Hackett, the other by Thomas Carew. The two boats now manned by Barbarian pirates, joined the ships and continued westward.

Captain Rais demanded that Hackett pilot them into Kinsale but it is believed that Hackett persuaded Captain Rais that Baltimore would be considerably easier to take. The pirates landed in the Baltimore Cove and at 2am that night they made their way inland. Once their feet touched the ground they purposefully and simultaneously torched the thatched roofs of the houses and wrestled sleeping villagers from their beds. Moving on to the main village, the pirates took more captives before William Harris, a local, fired a musket alerting the remaining villagers to the imminent attack. This persuaded Rais to retreat and end the raid. The pirates returned to the anchored ships with twenty men, thirty-three women and fifty-four children and set sail from the Baltimore coast to return to Algiers.

The British government would not provide funds for the release of the stolen men, women and children as they believed it would encourage further raiding. Once they were sold at slave auctions, men who had skills such as carpentry may have fared better than those who did not. For them a brutal life working in galleys or as labourers lay ahead. Women were sold as concubines and for the most part they were treated well. Children were apparently dealt with kindness but grew up to form a slave division of the Ottoman army unless they were bought and raised by a local family, when they were often treated as one of the family.

Back in Ireland in the aftermath of the raid the surviving villagers moved inland towards Skibbereen and the surrounding townlands in search of greater security. Hackett was later tried and condemned to death for his part in bringing the pirates to Baltimore.

Parklife
Dublin's Phoenix Park

Measuring 707 hectares the Phoenix Park in Dublin is one of Europe's largest enclosed parks and one of Ireland's most popular outdoor amenities. It was originally conceived as a Royal Deer Park in 1662 during the reign of King Charles II by Viceroy, James Butler, Duke of Ormond. It actually used to be even larger in size extending across the River Liffey as far as Kilmainham on Dublin's southside. Following construction of the Royal Hospital in Kilmainham the park boundaries were reduced. The entire park is now north of the Liffey. Dublin's postal districts are denoted by numbers: an odd number denotes the north side and an even number the south side. The Phoenix Park is in Dublin 8 making it the only northside address with an even postal district.

Almost one-third of the Phoenix Park is covered with deciduous trees including oak, ash, sycamore, beech and horse chestnut trees. It is so vast that the park supports 50 per cent of the mammal species found in Ireland and 40 per cent of the bird species. This includes a substantial fallow deer herd. The Phoenix Park has been home to Dublin Zoo since 1831, making it one of the oldest zoos in the world. It is now one of Ireland's busiest tourist attractions receiving over 900,000 visitors a year. In 1838 to celebrate Queen Victoria's coronation, the Zoo held an open day and over 20,000 people spilled through its gates. This still remains the highest number of visitors in a single day! In 1927 a lion called Cairbre was born in Dublin Zoo.

The Wellington Testimonial

He would go on to international fame as Leo the Lion, the logo for MGM film studios.

The Phoenix Park is also home to Europe's largest obelisk. Standing at 62.4 metres (205 feet), the Wellington Testimonial was designed by Robert Smirke and built to commemorate the victories of the Duke of Wellington.

Throughout the 20th century the Phoenix Park embraced its role as a park for the people and now has seven GAA pitches, three camogie pitches, twelve soccer pitches, two cricket pitches, and a model aeroplane arena is used by thousands of runners throughout the year in the Dublin City Marathon.

HOME SWEET HOME

The Phoenix Park is home to Ireland's president. Originally known as Ranger's Lodge, Áras an Uachtaráin was built in 1751 by Chief Ranger and Master of Game, Nathaniel Clements. It was later bought for the sum of £25,000 for use by the Royal Viceroy until the Irish Free State was established in 1922 and it became the residence of the Governor General. In 1938 Ireland's first president Douglas Hyde took up temporary residence in the viceregal lodge, which had been renamed Áras an Uachtaráin meaning 'House of the President'. With the outbreak of World War II the house became the President's permanent residence and when Sean T. Ó Ceallaigh succeeded Hyde as President a refurbishment programme was put in place. As home of the President of Ireland, the Áras has received dignitaries from all over the world. Some have even planted trees in the grounds. In 1963 John F. Kennedy planted a Wellingtonia; in 2011 President Barack Obama

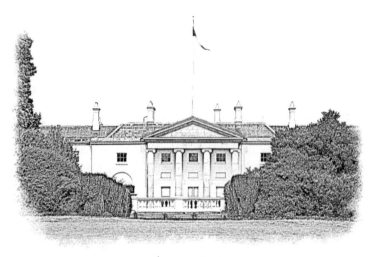

Áras an Uachtaráin

planted an oak tree. That same year, Queen Elizabeth became the first monarch in 100 years to visit Ireland and planted an oak tree at the Peace Bell in the Áras gardens. The Peace Bell was unveiled by Mary McAleese in 2008 to mark the tenth anniversary of the Good Friday Agreement. Each Irish president has also planted a tree in the grounds of the Phoenix Park residence.

A pint of the black stuff
A history of Irish stout

The creamy pint of stout that is so synonymous with Ireland actually originated in London in the 1720s. It soon made its way across the waters and into Irish taverns and alehouses. By 1800, porter as it was originally called had cemented its position as Ireland's favourite beer. Some of the reason for this lay in the fact that porter was cheaper to produce and hence, cheaper to buy. Brewers could use barley and hops of a lesser quality than that used in ale and because of the brewing methods used the quality of the porter was not compromised. The appearance of porter on the market coincided with a growth in the mass production and export of commodities. Unlike ale, porter actually travelled well and improved with age making it the ideal export commodity.

The growth of the London breweries coincided with stricter regulations and taxes around brewing and distilling in Ireland. Ireland had a history of small breweries and the threat of the excise inspector saw the demise of many of these small-scale producers. Irish makers of porter also paid more taxes than their English counterparts. As a result Irish consumers turned to porter from the big London breweries such as Whitbread and Truman. Within fifty years there was a major turnaround as brewing in Ireland was revitalised and

Arthur Guinness (1725–1803) and the Cork Porter Brewery entered the market.

Arthur Guinness had grown up in the brewing industry. Following the death of his mother, his father had remarried the owner of a local Inn at which there was a brewery. In 1755 Arthur and his brother Richard leased a brewery and supplied beer to the Castletown Estate in County Kildare. Four years later Arthur left Kildare for Dublin where he married Olivia Whitmore. Later that year, on 31 December 1759 Arthur Guinness signed a 9,000 year lease on a disused brewery at St James' Gate, Dublin. Guinness began by brewing ale but started producing porter due to its growing popularity. Porter consisted of four main ingredients, malted barley, hops, water and brewer's yeast. It was not long until Guinness was exported into England and St James' Gate concentrated on porter alone. Arthur Guinness brewed different types of porter to suit different tastes, including a special export beer called 'West India Porter'. This beer is still brewed today and is now known as Guinness Foreign Extra Stout. Arthur Guinness died in 1803 leaving a very successful brewing business in the hands of his son, Arthur Guinness II. The Guinness dynasty continued to be passed from father to son for five generations. Arthur II spearheaded the expansion of Guinness into foreign markets including America and Africa. Under Arthur II Guinness Extra Stout was produced specifically for the English market. This is also still produced today and is often referred to as Original Guinness. By 1868 Guinness was the largest brewery in the world. It was floated on the London Stock Exchange becoming the first ever brewery to be incorporated. Ten million glasses of Guinness are enjoyed daily in over 150 countries around the world. The site at St James' Gate is now an interactive museum and Ireland's most visited tourist attraction.

Bliain an áir: the year of the slaughter
The Famine of 1740–41

Prior to the Great Famine (1845–51), Ireland had been decimated by famine in 1741. In fact, in *'the year of the slaughter'* as it came to be known, between 310,000 and 480,000 people died of causes relating to famine. This was a greater percentage of the population in a shorter period of time than during the Great Famine a century later. Because there was no mass emigration following *'the year of the slaughter'* the population did not continue to drop in the same way that it did following the Great Famine.

Throughout the 1730s Ireland experienced mild winters but this all changed n 1739 when a *'great frost'* descended across the country. By January 1740 the rivers Liffey, Boyne, Slaney, Lee, Foyle and sections of the Shannon had frozen over. At first, the phenomenon was greeted as a novelty, particularly among the middle and upper classes. Apparently a hurling match was played on the frozen River Shannon and an outdoor fair was held in Cork on the frozen River Lee. For the poorer sectors of the population the novelty soon wore off. Fuel prices soared and many people died from hypothermia. When the thaw came in early February it was found that the extreme cold had destroyed virtually every potato in the country; this meant that there were no potatoes to provide seedlings for the coming year. The potato had recently been introduced to Ireland. As a crop it was cheap to harvest and had quickly gained popularity becoming the main crop and source of nourishment for a large portion of the population.

The poor climate continued into the summer of 1740 with Ireland experiencing a parching, dry and bitterly cold summer. This resulted in the death of cattle and the demise of any crops that had managed to survive the Great Frost. People were dying from dysentery and typhus resulting from famine. A relief scheme was set up by Lord Justice Hugh Boulter, Archbishop of

Armagh, in Dublin in January 1741 to feed the starving people of the city. By April that year with help from funds raised by Jonathan Swift, Dean of St Patrick's Cathedral and other noblemen, Lord Justice Hugh Boulter was feeding 4,400 Dubliners a day. Other schemes were carried out in Waterford and Kildare. The obelisk and remains of a wall surrounding Killiney Hill were originally constructed in 1742 by John Mapas in a bid to provide employment for those affected by the famine. A similar project was conceived by Lady Katherine Connolly at Castletown House in Leixlip as a means of income for those suffering in that locality. In September a series of storms and floods ravaged the country and at last the weather settled leaving behind it a country racked by famine and disease.

A MESSIAH ON THE STREETS OF DUBLIN

The Charitable Musical Society proposed to raise funds for famine relief activities in Dublin by inviting renowned German composer George Frideric Handel (1685–1759) to the city for a charity concert. Handel's last oratorio had been poorly received in England and wracked by debt and depression the composer was glad of the invitation. He arrived in Dublin in November 1741 giving his first performance at Neal's Musick, Fishamble Street on 23 December. He was warmly received by Dublin's high society and remained in the city to complete the Messiah, *a piece which he had began work on that summer. Rehearsals began the following February with choirs from St*

Patrick's and Christ Church Cathedrals. By 11 o'clock on the morning of the performance the Musick Hall was filled with over 700 wealthy patrons. Such was the demand for tickets that women were asked to forgo fashion for the day and leave their dress hoops at home. So successful was the performance that Handel performed again on 3 June 1742. He returned to England later that summer to critical acclaim. Handel and the performers had offered their services free of charge. All monies raised as a result of the performance went towards feeding those affected by the devastating famine.

To the White House
Ireland and the US presidency

Over twenty US presidents have or claim to have Irish roots. President John F. Kennedy (1917–1963), the 35th president was the first serving president to visit Ireland in June 1963. His visit was part of a wider European tour which took in Berlin where he gave his famous '*Ich bin ein Berliner*' speech. On the night of his arrival in Ireland he drove through the city in a motorcade and was greeted

John F. Kennedy

by thousands of well-wishers. He travelled on to his ancestral home in Dunganstown, County Wexford and became the first foreign leader to address the Houses of the Oireachtais in Dáil Éireann. Five months later he was assassinated in Dallas. Since his visit many American presidents have visited Ireland – in May 2011 Barack Obama and First Lady Michelle Obama were greeted by hundreds of people in the small village of Moneygall, Co. Offaly, Barack Obama's ancestral town. Presidents Richard Nixon, Ronald Reagan and the Bush family can also trace their ancestry back to Ireland.

President Andrew Jackson (1767–1845), the seventh American president, is perhaps the most Irish president of them all. His parents emigrated from County Antrim to South Carolina in 1765 and Andrew was born two years later. His father died shortly before his birth and when he was in his early teens his eldest brother was killed during the American Revolution (1775–83). Andrew was left without parents or siblings at the age of

The White House

fifteen following the death of his mother and two brothers from smallpox. Brought up by his uncles, Andrew Jackson went on to study law, rising through the ranks of his profession and later the US military.

In 1824 as a result of his military prowess, Jackson was nominated by a Pennsylvania convention to run for the American presidency. Despite winning the popular vote, Jackson was defeated by Democratic-Republican John Quincy Adams (1767–1848). The manner in which Jackson lost caused a split in the Democratic-Republican party. Those who supported Jackson called themselves the Democrats. Those who opposed him dubbed him 'Jackass'. Andrew embraced the nickname adopting an image of a donkey to represent himself. Andrew was nominated as Democratic presidential candidate three years prior to the next election and in 1828 he became the first Democratic president of the United States. He would go on to serve two terms. By the end of the 19th century the symbol of the donkey was synonymous with the Democrats and is still used today.

THE HOUSE THAT HOBAN BUILT

James Hoban (c.1755–1831), was born into the family of a tenant farmer in Callan, Co.Kilkenny on the land of the first Earl of Desart, Otway Cuffe. Cuffe had established a school on his estate so the tenants' children could receive an education. It is here that the young Hoban learnt to read, write and other skills such as carpentry and stone-masonry. Hoban's talent was spotted and Cuffe provided patronage for his further education at the Dublin Society Drawing School.

In the early 1780s Hoban emigrated to America where he forged a career in architecture, working on buildings first in Philadelphia and then Charleston, North Carolina where he worked on two of the city's most prominent buildings, a 1,200 seat theatre and the conversion of a colonial house into a court house. In 1792 President George Washington (1732–1799) opened a public competition to design the Executive Mansion or what would later become known as the White House. A French architect, Pierre L'Enfant, had earlier been granted the contract but his extravagant design proved too expensive to execute.

Inspired by Leinster House in Dublin, Hoban submitted his design and after meeting with President Washington and increasing the buildings size by thirty per cent Hoban was chosen as the architect of what would become one of the world's most recognizable buildings.

Probably the most famous glass in the world
Waterford Crystal

The Waterford Crystal story began in 1783 when brothers William and George Penrose successfully petitioned Parliament for aid in establishing a glass manufacturing plant in Waterford city. The brothers noticed a growing desire among the upper and middle classes for ornamental and functional flint glass. Rapidly expanding overseas trade meant the introduction of new products into Europe. This was to benefit Waterford Crystal plant. The factory employed approximately sixty people including skilled craftsmen, glass blowers, cutters and engravers. Following William Penrose's death in 1796 the factory was sold and eventually closed in 1851 due in part to the introduction of debilitating customs and excise duties on the manufacture and exportation of glass. There would be no further production of glass in the city of Waterford until after World War II when a small factory was established in Ballytruckle.

Glass experts from all over Europe trained at the new location. Miroslav Havel, a Czechoslovakian designer studied the pattern books used by the Penrose brothers in the 18th century to create the look and feel that is now synonymous with Waterford Crystal.

As Waterford Crystal began to sell direct to an American market keen for quality Irish glass, the fortunes of the company began to rise.

Glass blower

By 1973 Waterford Crystal had relocated to new premises, the biggest of its kind in the world. In 1986 they joined forces with Wedgwood, the prestigious North Staffordshire company renowned for its ceramics. However by the late 1980s falling demand and the declining US dollar meant that Waterford Wedgwood faced challenging times. The company changed ownership several times culminating in an agreement with Waterford City Council to open a new manufacturing and retail facility in the middle of the city giving the brand and the city a much-needed boost.

In 2010 the new *House of Waterford Crystal* opened and it is now a hugely popular tourist attraction with visitors flocking to see the processes involved in creating the beautiful glass admired the world over.

Waterford Crystal has produced trophies for the French and German Grand Prixs, the Tennis Master series, The Volvo Ocean Race and the American National College Football Championship.

Perhaps one of the most exciting commissions was the famous New York City ball drop, which was designed and executed by Waterford Crystal for the Millennium celebrations. Although much of the glass is now produced outside Ireland it will always be synonymous with its home in the city of Waterford.

NOTHING IS CERTAIN EXCEPT FOR DEATH AND TAXES

In 1746 a glass tax was introduced in Great Britain and Ireland. This tax affected all glass sold and was based on weight. In a bid to promote the glass manufacturing industry in Ireland the tax was abolished in 1780. The success of Waterford Crystal is testament to the success of the initiative. However the Glass Tax was re-introduced in 1825 and endured, despite protests, until 1851.

Stand up and be counted
Ireland's Census

In Ireland the census currently takes place every five years with the purpose of gathering information about the general population. The information gathered presents a picture of the population; its housing conditions and demographic, social and economic characteristics. The information collected includes data on age, gender, country of origin, marital status, housing conditions, number of children, education, employment, etc. Unlike gender, age, marital status, and occupation, religious affiliation is among the more marginal census variables. As such it is not included in every country's census. Religion played a major role in Ireland's relationship with Britain and has always been part of the Irish census.

A completed census was first undertaken in Ireland under British rule in 1821. Following this, censuses were conducted decennially. The 1911 census became the last census to be taken by British administration. As such it was the last census to include information for the entire island of Ireland. Partition of the island of Ireland in 1921 meant that there was an interruption in the ten year pattern. The first census taken under the Free State was in 1926.

Monster Meetings!
Daniel O'Connell

After achieving Catholic Emancipation for Ireland in 1829 Daniel O'Connell (1775–1847) set his sights on repealing the Act Of Union, which in 1801 had merged the parliaments of Great Britain and Ireland to form the United Kingdom of Great Britain and Ireland. Prior to Catholic Emancipation, Catholics could not take a seat in the British Parliament as they had to swear allegiance to the British Monarch who was also head of the Protestant Church. Thanks to O'Connell, they no longer had to do this but many felt this was not enough.

O'Connell set about campaigning

for repeal of the Union. He took to the roads of Ireland on a tour taking in towns of historical significance such as Kells and Cashel, employing people power to bring about change in a non-violent manner. These meetings have developed legendary status over the centuries. They were given the moniker '*monster meetings*' in honour of the thousands of people who flocked to hear 'the Liberator' speak.

The monster meetings were more than just large rallies in fields around the country. They were full-on spectacles. Almost every meeting began with a grand parade, often a few miles in length. They contained brass bands, floats and carts, followed by thousands of people from the surrounding areas on foot or horseback. The procession would make its way out from the city or town to greet O'Connell and escort him back through the streets to a field or wide open area. Once in place O'Connell would give a rousing speech urging his followers to demand that the union be repealed. Once the speeches were over O'Connell was usually brought out to enjoy an evening banquet with the local hierarchy.

Estimations for the number of people that attended the monster meetings range anywhere from 100,000 to 1,000,000. If we were to take the lowest possible estimated number of attendees per meeting it would mean that throughout his tour of Ireland about 1,500,000 people came out to join O'Connell's mass meetings. This type of mass people-power

Daniel O'Connell

without violence was unique in Europe at this time.

More importantly was the buzz that was created around O'Connell. Newspapers throughout Ireland and the United Kingdom reported on the size of the meetings and what O'Connell said to his supporters. Although this roused the people around him it was also for the benefit of the politicians who would read reports of the evening's events in the newspapers the following day.

The biggest meeting yet was set for Clontarf in County Dublin. This was the spot where Brian Boru, the most famous High King of Ireland (c.941–1014) had defeated the Vikings. However, on 7 October 1843 Robert Peel (1788–1850), the British Prime Minister, issued a statement banning the meeting. Troops were deployed from mainland Britain to ensure that the rally did not go ahead. Throughout his campaign O'Connell had remained non-violent and within the confines of the law. He was not prepared to jeopardize himself or his followers. He made the decision to call a halt to what would have been the biggest monster meeting the country had ever seen. Posters were put up around the city announcing the cancellation. Activists on horseback travelled the sidestreets urging those already heading to Dublin to retreat. The cancelling of the meeting signalled the end of O'Connell's time as an inspiring orator and a change of direction for Irish activists was imminent.

THE TEMPERANCE MOVEMENT

Had Daniel O'Connell's monster meetings taken place a century earlier in Ireland, perhaps they may not have gone by so smoothly. Throughout the 18th century, fairs, wakes and any sort of social gatherings held in Ireland were synonymous with alcohol, particularly a potent home-brew known as poitín. Led by Fr. Theobald Mathew (1790–1856), from Cork, a growing temperance movement spread throughout urban and rural Ireland. Five million people out of a population of 8.2 million took the teetotal pledge. Daniel O'Connell himself even pledged to give up the booze in 1840! As the century progressed and the Great Famine began mass teetotalism went by the wayside.

Ireland's national necropolis
Glasnevin Cemetery

Glasnevin cemetery is the final resting place for more than 1.5 million people. There are more people beneath the ground of the cemetery than there are walking the streets of Dublin. The cemetery opened in 1832 following action by Daniel O'Connell who recognized the need for a graveyard where Catholics could bury their dead. Following the reformation and the appropriation of the Catholic Church's land, Catholics had been forced to bury their dead in Protestant graveyards, paying fees to Protestant ministers. O'Connell campaigned and following the passing of the '*Easement of Burial*

Bills' in 1824, a committee was established and four years later land was obtained at Goldenbridge in Dublin. The first burial took place on the 15 October of that year. Due to the increasing population in 1831, more land was secured at Glasnevin. Originally called Prospect Cemetery, the 124 acre site soon became known as Glasnevin Cemetery. Michael Carey, an eleven year old boy who died of tuberculosis was the first person to be buried there on 22 February 1832.

The high walls and watch towers that surround the graveyards although decorative in appearance were actually a necessity in 19th century Dublin. Grave robbing and body-snatching were rife in the city. Medical colleges required vast numbers of bodies for dissection and paid handsomely for any they received. Some wily criminals viewed body-snatching as an opportunity to make money and targeted Glasnevin Cemetery in particular. The passing of the Anatomy Act in 1832 provided a legal source of bodies for medical research and grave-robbing rates declined.

Many prominent figures from Irish history are buried at Glasnevin, Daniel O'Connell, Maud Gonne, Constance Markievicz, Cathal Brugha, James Larkin, Eamon de Valera and Christy Brown to name but a few. Roger Casement's remains were repatriated to Ireland almost fifty years after he was hanged in Pentonville Prison for Treason following his part in the 1916 Easter Rising. He was given a state funeral on 1 March 1965 and buried in the Republican Plot with others who fought for Ireland's freedom.

The funeral of Charles Stewart Parnell remains the biggest funeral ever witnessed at Glasnevin cemetery. Over a quarter of a million people lined the streets. Train companies put on special trains so that mourners from throughout Ireland could travel to Dublin to pay their respects. The streets were thronged with crowds of people following the funeral procession to Glasnevin Cemetery. When Michael Collins died tickets had to be issued for the funeral. His grave remains the most visited at the cemetery. Fresh flowers arrive daily along with a stream of cards on Valentine's Day for the 'Big Fellow'.

MY HEART TO ROME, MY BODY TO IRELAND AND MY SOUL TO HEAVEN
Those were the last wishes of 'the Liberator' Daniel O'Connell, and appear in gold above his family crypt at Glasnevin Cemetery. While on a pilgrimage to Rome, O'Connell died in Genoa. He requested that his heart be taken to Rome and the rest of his body to Ireland. He was interred in a specially commissioned crypt in Glasnevin Cemetery.
The O'Connell crypt features a black Kilkenny marble altar and contains the remains of O'Connell and eight members of his immediate family, including sons, daughters and grandchildren. The crypt lies beneath a 51 metre (168 foot) round tower designed by George Petrie and built between

---

Sackville Street

The Unsung Hero
Ireland's Antarctic explorer

Daniel O'Connell

1855 and 1869. Its construction was funded by public subscriptions. It was built around the same time as the Wellington Monument in Phoenix Park and Nelson's Pillar on the then Sackville Street, now O'Connell Street. It was damaged by a suspected loyalist bomb attack in 1971 in reprise for the destruction of Nelson's Pillar by republican activists on O'Connell Street. This resulted in the monument being closed to the public until recent years.

Tom Crean (1877–1938) was one of ten children born into an impoverished family of farmers outside the small Kerry village of Annascaul on the Dingle Peninsula. Like most boys from his background he left school at an early age with basic reading and writing skills. At the age of fifteen he enlisted in the British Naval Forces. He would go on to feature on more polar expeditions than any other explorer of his generation.

Tom Crean's life as an explorer began when he joined Robert Falcon Scott's (1868–1912) Discovery expedition in 1901. Ernest Shackleton (1874–1922) was also a member of the crew. On the Discovery expedition Crean was one of a group of twelve men who stood at 79° 15' S. This was the furthest south any humans had ever reached. Scott, Shackleton and Edward Wilson travelled ahead in a bid to reach the elusive South Pole. The remaining crew members returned to camp. The three-man team made it to 82° 17' S, before conditions forced them to abandon the quest but Scott remained determined to conquer the Pole. A decade later Crean returned with Scott on his doomed 1911 Polar expedition. He was a key figure on the expedition, pulling a sledge to within 150 miles of the South Pole before being ordered by Scott to return to base camp. On the return journey Crean's companion, Lieutenant Evans, collapsed from scurvy and exhaustion. Crean took it upon himself to go for help. He took off with no sleeping bag, two pieces of chocolate and three biscuits. His solitary trek lasted eighteen hours and saved the life of his companion. Meanwhile, on 17 January, Scott and the remaining crew members reached the Pole. To their utter dismay a Norwegian party, led by Roald Amundsen, had beaten them to it. They had no choice but to begin the perilous 1,500 km journey back. Scott died of starvation and exposure in a tent on 29 March 1912. He was only 11 km (6.8 miles) from a pre-arranged food depot. The bodies of Scott

and his fellow explorers were later discovered and buried by Crean and the remaining crew. Evans would go on to dedicate his biography to William Lashly who had remained behind with him and Tom Crean who had gone for help. For this act of bravery the men received the Albert Medal.

Less than one year after returning from the ill-fated Terra Nova expedition, Tom Crean returned to Antarctica again, this time with Shackleton. Shackleton was leading the *Endurance* expedition on the Imperial Trans-Antarctic Expedition, attempting to walk across the frozen continent, from coast to coast, via the South Pole. Tom Crean joined the expedition as Second Officer. He was the only man, from a crew of more than thirty, that had travelled on the previous expedition to return to Antarctica.

The *Endurance* ship was crushed and trapped by pack ice in the Weddell Sea before the explorers got an opportunity to set foot on Antarctic shores. Weeks turned into months as the men remained trapped. Eventually Shackleton decided to sail for help and leave the majority of his crew on Elephant Island, living under upturned lifeboats to protect them from the harshest of weather. He set sail with Frank Worsley and Tom Crean in a small lifeboat, the James Caird, across the Southern Ocean. At last they landed at South Georgia but unfortunately on the unpopulated side and so faced a hazardous trek of 64km (40 miles) across mountainous terrain to the nearest whaling station. It was so arduous that Shackleton later remarked that there were four of us walking the journey, meaning that he felt the presence of God

with them. When they arrived at the whaling station they were not recognized at first as they had changed so drastically. Once recovered, Shackleton sailed back to Elephant Island to rescue his crew, all who had survived by catching birds and seals. Despite requests from Shackleton, it was Crean's last trip to the Antarctic region.

Tom Crean continued to serve in the British navy throughout World War I until his retirement in 1920. He returned to an Ireland in turmoil. It is believed that this is one of the reasons so little was known about his time as an explorer. As Ireland fought for independence many would not have looked favourably on a man who had travelled to the Antarctic under the British flag. Crean opened a bar, The South Pole Inn, with his wife near the place of his birth and worked there until his death from appendicitis in 1938. It was not until a groundbreaking biography entitled *Unsung Hero* by Michael Smith was published in 2000 that the true extent of Crean's involvement in the Antarctic explorations was revealed.

Keogh's Last Stand
Myles Keogh and the Battle of Little Big Horn

Born in Leighlinbridge in Carlow on 25 March 1840, Myles Walter Keogh was one of 1,400 Irishmen who in March 1860, answered the call of Pope Pius IX to join the Papal army in a bid to keep hold of the Papal States. For his part in the failed mission Keogh was awarded two papal decorations, for participation in the siege of the Adriatic port city of Ancona in Italy. From Italy, he was recruited to fight on the Union side in the US Civil War. He served at the battles of Fredericksburg and Chancellorsville. He was decorated with the brevet rank of major for his efforts in the battle of Gettysburg. 10,000 soldiers were stationed in the American West and there was a huge Irish contingent in the army. Approximately 2,500 of these men were born in Ireland. As a result of mass emigration because of the Great Famine they had headed for America and many joined the army.

Captain Myles Keogh (standing)

Following the Civil War Keogh applied for a commission in the regular US army. He went on to take part in over eighty engagements and became a captain in the newly formed 7th US Cavalry led by General George Armstrong Custer. 126 of the 822 soldiers in the regiment were Irish-born. They were charged with keeping the peace on the great American Plains and ensuring that the Native Americans like the Lakota, better known as the Sioux, the Cheyenne, and the Blackfeet, remained in their defined reservations.

On 25 June 1876 Captain Myles Walter Keogh, commanding officer of Company 'I' of the 7th Cavalry was one of 268 US cavalrymen wiped out by the Native Americans at the Battle of Little Bighorn. As a result of reckless action by their leader, Custer, 268 soldiers lost their lives. Custer completely miscalculated by sending 600 men against a Native American village that contained up to 5,000 men. He divided his command and everyone who went with Custer lost their lives. The only survivor was Keogh's horse Comanche. Keogh was senior captain among the five companies massacred with Custer. He died surrounded by his fellow soldiers just a few hundred yards away from Last Stand Hill where Custer died. All the bodies were scalped and mutilated except for those of Custer and Keogh. It is believed the Sioux may have found the decoration

conferred on Keogh by the Pope and been wary of its powers as they themselves wore decorative jewellery to ward off evil spirits.

Captain Myles Keogh was buried in New York State but at the site of Custer's Last Stand there is a gravestone bearing his name. Keogh's horse, Comanche, the only survivor of the battle on the army's side, was badly injured and found days later when reinforcements eventually arrived. When Comanche finally died he was stuffed and is now housed in the University of Kansas Natural History Museum.

Green, white and orange
The significance of the tricolour

The national flag of Ireland is a tricolour of green, white and orange. The tricolour was first flown publicly in Waterford City on 7 March 1848 by Thomas Francis Meagher (1823–1867), a leader of the Young Irelanders. He flew the flag from the Wolfe Tone Confederate Club, Waterford

City. There it remained flying for eight days and nights until it was eventually taken down by the British. Following that, the flag was flown at meetings all over the country, side by side with the French flag in solidarity for their hard fought revolution.

In April 1848, Meagher, William Smith O'Brien and Richard O'Gorman went to Paris to congratulate the French on overthrowing King Louis Philippe. While they were there, a group of French women wove an Irish tricolour from silk and presented it to Meagher. On his return to Ireland Meagher presented the silk flag to the citizens of Ireland, saying *'The white in the centre signifies a lasting truce between the 'orange' and the 'green'.'* The green represents Irish nationalism; the orange, Ireland's Protestant minority, and the Orange Order; the white, lasting peace between the two. Inspired by the revolutions taking place in Europe, Meagher led the Young Irelanders in a failed rebellion. For his part in the disturbance Meagher was later tried

for treason and sentenced to death. His sentence was commuted to banishment to Van Diemen's Land in Australia. He would later escape to the United States. Many years later, the tricolour was hung by the 1916 leaders from the top of the GPO. It was then used by the Irish Republican Army during the War of Independence (1919–1921) and by the Irish Free State before being written into the 1937 Constitution.

NATIONAL SYMBOL

The national symbol of Ireland is the harp. Ireland is the only country in the world to have a musical instrument as its national symbol. It appears on all Irish coins, is engraved on the seal of the office of the President and appears on the flag of the President of Ireland. The design of the harp is based on the 14th century Brian Boru Harp preserved in the Museum of Trinity College, Dublin. According to legend, Brian Boru played the harp the night before the Battle of Clontarf in 1014. In reality; the instrument is

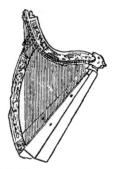

The Irish Harp

dated a few centuries after Brian Boru's time. The harp has been recognized as a national symbol of Ireland from as early as the 13th century.

'Til death do us part...
Costello Memorial Chapel

On the end of Bridge Street in Carrick-on-Shannon County Leitrim sandwiched between two pubs stands the smallest church in Ireland and possibly the second smallest church in the world. Covering an area of just 28 metres (92 feet), the chapel is 4.8 metres (16 feet) long,

3.6 metres (12 feet) wide and 9.1 metres (30 feet) high. This minute chapel was built in 1879 by Edward Costello following the untimely death of his wife, Mary Josephine Costello at the age of forty-six on 6 October 1877. Broken-hearted, Edward commissioned the building of the chapel as a final resting place for his beloved wife. The body of Mary Josephine Costello was embalmed following her death and placed in the care of local nuns who had recently come to Carrick-on-Shannon and set up a school for girls.

The church is built entirely from stone with a single stained-glass window to the rear, below which stands a marble altar. The entrance is marked by two stone pillars topped by Celtic crosses. The Costello coat of arms is visible at the top of the gable. The Latin words translate to; '*Seek not thyself outside thyself*'.

On completion of the church in April 1879 Mary Costello's coffin was lowered into a sunken area to the left of the entrance door and her coffin covered with reinforced glass. Mass was celebrated every first

Costello Chapel

Friday in the Chapel from consecration until the death of Mr Costello in March 1891. He was buried in the same manner across from his beloved wife to the right handside of the chapel entrance. Referred to locally as Ireland's Taj Mahal, the small chapel remains a monument to love in the heart of County Leitrim.

THE RED-HEADED REBEL

Susan Langstaff Mitchell (1866–1926) was born in Carrick-on-Shannon on 6 December 1866. Her father was manager of the town's Provincial Bank. She was the fifth of seven children and when her father died in 1872 the large family was split up. Susan was sent to live with aunts on Wellington Road in Dublin and grew up to be one of Ireland's pioneering women. While most women of her social standing were expected to marry well and have children, Susan concentrated on her burgeoning writing career. She took up a position as assistant editor at the **Irish Homestead**, *a weekly magazine containing articles, poetry and short stories. James Joyce's first short story was published on its pages. Mitchell was the face behind 'Brigid', a pseudonym for the magazine's 'Household Hints' columnist. She used this column as a platform from which to engage in debate about the changing roles of women in Irish society. Mitchell was a keen satirist and produced three volumes of* *poetry in her lifetime, never shying away from issues close to her heart. She died on 4 March 1926, and her funeral was attended by Jack B Yeats, WB Yeats, Douglas Hyde, Lord Dunsany, and Sarah Purser. On 1 October 2016 a bronze bust of Mitchell was unveiled in Carrick-on-Shannon celebrating the 150th anniversary of the birth of this important literary figure.*

'We are Alcock and Brown. Yesterday we were in America.'
The first transatlantic flight

At 8.40am on Sunday 15 June 1919 Captain John Alcock and Lieutenant Arthur Whitten Brown landed their Vickers Vimy airplane in a bog near Clifden in County Galway. They were the first ever people to complete a non-stop trans-Atlantic flight between America and Europe. This historic event was the result of a competition conceived in 1913 by Lord Northcliffe, proprietor of the British newspaper, the *Daily Mail*.

The newspaper offered a prize of £10,000 to the first aviators to cross the Atlantic non-stop in under seventy-two hours. Following the outbreak of World War I, the competition was suspended until 1918.

By the spring of 1919, several teams had gathered in St John's, Newfoundland in a bid to become the first to cross the Atlantic and collect the prize money. Following a chance meeting Alcock persuaded Brown to join him in his bid to make history. Their late entry into the competition ensured that they were viewed as outsiders.

Their chosen mode of transport was a Vickers Vimy. This was a twin engine bomber, originally developed to be used as a fighter plane during the war. It had a wingspan of over 20 metres (67 feet) and was 13.05 metres (42.8 feet) long. It was fitted with two 360hp Rolls-Royce Eagle VIII engines and was capable of travelling at ninety miles per hour. The actual airplane used for the record-setting attempt was modified by removing the bomb racks and

Vickers Vimy

adding additional fuel tanks. Once the plane was assembled, a suitable runway cleared and the inclement weather passed, the pilot and navigator waited eagerly in an open cockpit at the front of the airplane ready for takeoff. Alcock and Brown lifted off from Lester's Field on the afternoon of 14 June. Not long into the flight the daring duo's transmitter failed leaving them unable to communicate with anyone on the ground.

It was a difficult flight; the bad weather that hindered their departure did not improve, with rain turning into snow the further east they flew. Eventually Alcock and Brown spotted land; Eeshal island and then Turbot Island off the Galway coast; they had reached Ireland. Spotting the tall masts of the Marconi wireless station at Derrygimla, south of Clifden, Alcock landed the plane in what he presumed was a field but which was in fact marshy bog, resulting in the aircraft nose-diving into the ground. The damage to the Vimy was minimal and the airmen stepped out unhurt and victorious onto Irish soil. The groundbreaking 1,900 mile flight had taken sixteen hours and twenty-seven minutes.

The *Daily Mail* had a special correspondent ensconced on Ireland's West Coast awaiting the arrival of the first non-stop transatlantic flight but he was pipped at the post by the editor of the *Connacht Tribune*, T.J.W. Kenny, who got to Derrygimla first. The wily reporter sold the story internationally such was the interest in Alcock and Brown's amazing feat.

Before leaving Ireland for England, the pioneering aviators were greeted by hordes of well-wishers in every town on their journey. A Galway jeweller even presented them with Claddagh rings. On arrival in London, Alcock and Brown were awarded the prize money by the British Secretary of State for War and Air, Winston Churchill. The following week they were knighted by King George V.

A monument to mark the historic landing site now stands at Errislannon overlooking Derrygimla bog. The inscription reads: *'Ta a ngaisce greannta as chlar na speire. Their heroism adorns the expanses of the sky'*.

Watch the tram car please
Ireland's trams

Georgian Dublin was an accessible city, contained within two canals. It was relatively easy to walk from one side of Dublin to the other and necessary as public transport was all but non-existent. By the end of the 19th century all that had changed. The city was criss-crossed with electric tramlines taking the city's inhabitants around the city and out into the suburbs.

In February 1872 the first Dublin horse tram ran, operating between College Green and Garville Avenue in Rathgar. The double-decker trams were pulled by two horses. Both the driver and the passengers sat on the top deck. Originally the trams served mainly a middle-class clientele travelling on the Southside of the city before eventually travelling out as far as Clontarf, a seaside suburb on Dublin's Northside.

In May 1896 the first electric tram was operated from Haddington Road to Dalkey, a Southside coastal location by the Dublin Southern District Tramways Company. By January 1901 electrification of all Dublin's tramways was in full swing and the end of horse-powered trams was announced.

Dublin trams could reach a speed of 40mph on straight routes making it a very efficient means of transport. However, the introduction of the car to Irish roads and their growth in popularity in the 1920s, together with the newly designed four-wheeled bogey bus, hailed the end of the tram on Dublin's streets. The last tram in Dublin city ran on 9 July 1949. The Howth Head tram line lasted another ten years before taking its last journey. In the run up to its demise an unprecedented number of commuters travelled on the Hill of Howth trams taking in the breathtaking scenery on this unique form of transport At the height of its use, Dublin United Tramways was the seventh largest tram system in Europe, with 330 tram cars, yet of all the trams that made up the urban landscape during the 20th century, only five remain in Ireland's transport museum.

Other urban electric tramways ran in Belfast and Cork. In Cork, the trams were of the open top and open front design and were abandoned around 1931. An industrial tramway ran from the town of Newry to serve working mills at Bessbrook. This system, which closed in 1948, was entirely single deck in design and was the first in the world to use the bow system of current connection, which was later used world-wide.

One of the most incredible

The Giant's Causeway Tram

electric tramway systems in the world was the Giant's Causeway tram. The route it took along the scenic Antrim Coast was unbelievably picturesque. It ran for 65 years before finally closing in 1949.

After lifting the tracks from the city's streets and de-railing the beautiful tramcars, Ireland's capital city has once again embraced the tram, albeit a sleeker, modernised version. The Luas began transporting passengers across Dublin city and out to the suburbs in 2004 to help alleviate congestion on Dublin's busy roads.

Armagh

FROM THE GREEN, GREEN GRASS OF HOME TO THE STREETS OF NEW YORK

The first ever street tramway system was introduced to New York by an Irishman, John Stephenson (1809–1893). Stephenson emigrated from Armagh to the States where he worked as a coach builder. He invented and patented the tramcar which was originally hauled by steam until horses were introduced. In 1832 it became the first horse-tramway system in the world, running from Prince Street to 14th Street and providing a fifteen minute service over a four mile route. The tram could carry thirty passengers.

Boycott!
The Land League

The long depression was a period of worldwide recession which began in 1873 and lasted until the late 1890s. It was particularly devastating for small-scale Irish farmers and producers of food and beer. Paper-making, rope-making and tanning which had been integral to employment in small towns all but disappeared. A new railway system that covered most of the country meant that mass-produced products were readily available country-wide. As the worldwide depression deepened demand for Irish butter and beef in Britain was at an all-time low. As a result both small and large-scale tenant farmers were struggling to pay their rents. All across Ireland thousands faced eviction. The horrendous weather conditions in the summer of 1879 coupled with the return of potato blight brought the situation to a head. As well as the fear of losing their homes and livelihoods, many families were on the brink of starvation.

Michael Davitt (1846–1906), the son of a small tenant farmer from Mayo had moved to England with his family as a young boy. After losing his arm in a cotton-milling accident, Davitt returned to school and completed his education going on to become a journalist. He maintained an interest in Irish politics and was an active member of the Irish Republican Brotherhood or IRB, a small, secret revolutionary organization whose sole goal was to establish a free, independent Ireland. Returning to Mayo, following a stint in America, Davitt was shocked at the level of destitution. He joined forces with the Fenians in organizing local farmers to mount mass demonstrations against a local landlord. This resulted in reduced rates for a number of tenants. The success of this rally encouraged other tenants to follow suit. Davitt was shrewd enough to realise that by harnessing the support of the farmers he could gain national support for Irish independence. He encouraged Charles Stewart Parnell (1846–1891), to join him

in Westport, County Mayo where Parnell gave a rousing speech encouraging tenant farmers to fight for fair rents. Following this rally, Davitt founded the Land League of Mayo. It was not long before similar organizations began to pop up throughout the country, resulting in the formation of the Irish National Land League with Parnell as its president.

The success of the Land League lay in the fact that all levels of society were affected by unfair treatment by landlords. Unlike its mainly Fenian membership, Parnell advocated non-violent agitation in achieving his aims. He urged tenant farmers to shun the landlords who evicted them and for others to do the same. The success of such peaceful means of protest was seen most clearly in Lough Mask, Co. Mayo and even gave rise to a new word in the English language: Boycott.

Captain Charles Boycott presided over a vast estate in Co. Mayo. Following a spate of bad weather resulting in ruined crops, Captain Boycott served eviction orders to a number of his tenants.

Servants, blacksmiths and farm-hands refused to work for him; local shopkeepers refused to serve him. In frustration Captain Boycott wrote to the *London Times* looking for help. Loyalists in Ireland rallied to support him and the *Belfast News-Letter* started a campaign for re-enforcements to assist Captain Boycott with harvesting his crops. Orangemen from Counties Monaghan and Cavan headed for Ballinrobe by train.

The story had garnered international interest and reporters that flocked to this remote Irish village from as far afield as the United States were disappointed to discover that no violence broke out. The Land Leaguers followed their instructions to the letter, remaining calm but resolute in their defiance of Captain Boycott.

Despite torrential rainfall, the Orangemen lifted the necessary crops. The cost of this act of support for Captain Boycott far outweighed that of the value of the crops and although on the face of it victory was Boycott's, in actual fact it was the moral protesters of the Land

League that were the true victors. Throughout Ireland any landlord that attempted to evict tenants was shunned or *'boycotted'* and evictions became less commonplace.

'I WILL GIVE MY LIFE TO IRELAND, BUT TO YOU I GIVE MY LOVE'
Hailed as 'the uncrowned king of Ireland' for the part he played in using politics to improve the lives of ordinary Irish men and women, Charles Stewart Parnell was unceremoniously kicked from his pedestal when one of the greatest Irish scandals of the 19th century was revealed. In December 1889, William O'Shea, formerly one of Parnell's most loyal supporters, filed for divorce from his wife Katherine on the grounds of her adultery with Parnell. Trapped in a loveless marriage, when Katherine or 'Kitty' met Parnell they fell madly in love. Theirs was a long-term affair and they were regularly seen out together in London. They had three children though they all bore O'Shea's name. Captain

Stranger than fiction
The story of Knock, Ireland's renowned Marian Shrine

Charles Stewart Parnell

O'Shea ignored the relationship as he was waiting to receive his portion of an inheritance from one of Kitty's aunts. When it became clear that he would not benefit from the inheritance he filed for divorce citing his wife's affair with Parnell as the reason. The divorce was played out in a public courtroom and Parnell was forced to resign from the Irish Parliamentary Party. On 25 June 1891 Parnell and O'Shea were married in a registry office. Parnell died from pneumonia in Kitty O'Shea's arms, just four short months after their marriage.

Ireland's answer to Lourdes, Fatima and Medjugorje is a Marian Shrine in an unassuming country village in County Mayo. The sun may not shine quite as often as it does in other European pilgrimage sites but since the Virgin Mary's apparition in 1879 Knock has remained a popular place of worship for Catholics, receiving over 1,500,000 visitors annually. This figure is calculated on the number of Communion hosts that are given out each year. Some visitors will come but will not receive Communion and others will receive Communion more than once. A similar system is used in Lourdes and Fatima.

On 21 August 1879 fifteen people, ranging in age from five to seventy-four, witnessed a vision at the gable wall of the local parish church in Knock. The fifteen locals attested to seeing an apparition of the Virgin Mary, St Joseph and St John the Evangelist. The latter was identified because he held a book while Mary was shrouded in white from head to toe and gazing upward as though deep in prayer. The vision occurred at eight o'clock and remained visible until half past nine. Although it was raining heavily the witnesses claimed that the area around the gable wall and the apparition remained dry. One witness went forward to kiss the feet of Mary but her embrace met with nothing but the wall. Mary did not utter a word, remaining silent throughout. This differentiates the apparition from those in Lourdes and Fatima where Mary engaged with those she appeared to.

There was undoubtedly some scepticism around the vision and so six weeks later Dr John MacHale, Archbishop of Tuam, held an Ecclesiastical Commission of Enquiry. Each of the fifteen witnesses was interviewed and a written statement taken. The Commission reported that they believed the witnesses' accounts to be 'trustworthy and satisfactory'. The town was declared a Marian Shrine and people began to visit

from near and far. Reporters came from all around the world to see the site where the Virgin Mary had appeared on a cold, wet August night in 1879.

The site grew in popularity in the latter half of the 20th century. This was in part due to the efforts of a local man, James Horan. Horan studied to be a priest at St Patrick's ecclesiastical college in Maynooth and in 1963 he took up a position in Knock, becoming Parish Priest two years later. He campaigned tirelessly for proper facilities at Knock. This culminated in the building of Knock Basilica in 1976 and a visit by Pope John Paul II in

Knock Basilica

1979. Nearly three million people turned out to welcome the pontiff at five different venues: Dublin's Phoenix Park, Drogheda, Galway, Limerick and Knock. No mean feat when you consider the country's total population in 1979 was 3,368,217. Knock had been given a very public seal of approval from the Head of the Catholic Church.

As recession hit Ireland in the 1980s record numbers of people emigrated from the West of Ireland. Monsignor Horan and a group of dedicated supporters strongly believed that the building of an airport at Knock could turn the fortunes of this pilgrim town around. State funding was agreed and when it temporarily ceased, Monsignor Horan and others from the local community raffled off land, houses, machinery and cattle to raise the required amount. Knock International Airport opened on 25 October 1985 with three Aer Lingus charter flights to Rome. In 2016 the airport welcomed its 10 millionth passenger.

Death of a language
How a generation tried to revive the Irish language

Following the fall of Charles Stewart Parnell, Ireland experienced something of a political lull. During this hiatus new movements emerged. Instead of politics, movements such as the Gaelic Athletic Association (GAA) and The Gaelic League were concerned with Ireland's cultural heritage and creating a sense of national identity and pride. Reclaiming the Irish language was central to this movement. The Tudor plantations of Ireland had forced Catholics off their land and compelled many Irish to relinquish their way of life from the religion they practiced to the language they spoke. This was cemented by centuries of oppression until Irish as a language was only spoken in some of the poorest and most remote parts of the country. As Ireland was under British rule, English was the country's official language and the language through which children were educated. Following the Great

Famine and the resulting fall in population, the decline of the Irish language continued. By the 1851 census less than a quarter of the population of Ireland spoke Gaelic. This was to fall further so that by 1901 it was as low as 14 per cent.

Growing nationalism created a realization that old Irish customs, folklore and the Gaelic language were what made Ireland unique. Many realised that to lose these characteristics of Irishness would be detrimental to Ireland's cultural legacy. The Gaelic League or *Conradh na Gaeilge* was formed by Douglas Hyde (1860–1949) and Eoin MacNeill (1867–1945) in 1893. Hyde had become fascinated by the Irish language whilst growing up in rural Roscommon listening to locals speak the language. MacNeill had grown up in Antrim in a community that had maintained some Irish language traditions. He would later visit the Aran Islands where Irish was the predominant language to improve his Gaelic speaking skills.

Hyde and McNeil's aim in setting up the Gaelic League was to encourage people to embrace the Irish language and Irish customs such as dance, story-telling and *Sean Nós* singing. Eugene O'Growney, a priest who studied at St Patrick's an Ecclesiastical college in Maynooth was also involved in setting up the League. O'Growney noticed the difficulties many had in learning Irish and published a series of lessons entitled *Simple Lessons in Irish* in the *Weekly Freeman*, a weekend newspaper. The series proved so popular that the lessons were compiled and published as a booklet. With this new-found interest in Gaelic language and culture membership of the Gaelic League began to steadily increase. New clubs began to sprout up throughout Ireland. By 1904 there were 600 Gaelic League clubs with over 50,000 members. Although many members improved their Gaelic skills through Irish language lessons the dances and sing-songs organized in towns throughout the country may have provided another reason for joining. Membership extended beyond Ireland to include the diaspora in England, America and as far afield as South Africa.

Although the Gaelic League was formed as a non-political, multi-denominational organization the fact that it promoted embracing Irish language and culture ensured it attracted members with strong nationalist views. Many of Ireland's future revolutionaries were members including Eamon de Valera, Patrick Pearse, Thomas MacDonagh and Roger Casement. Douglas Hyde's vision for the Gaelic League was a club that promoted inclusivity. As a Protestant he hoped that a shared love for the Irish language and customs would unite rather than divide Catholics and Protestants. As the 20th century progressed and Home Rule looked like a real prospect, separatist views grew among nationalist Gaelic League members changing the dynamic of the organization. Douglas Hyde resigned as president in 1915 citing ill-health. However, many believed that it was the increasing politicization of the Gaelic League which was responsible for his decision.

The role of the Gaelic League in reinvigorating the Irish language cannot be underestimated. Although the numbers of Irish speakers may not have increased the Gaelic League succeeded in restoring pride in the Irish language among the Irish people. The future leaders of the Irish Free State who were heavily influenced by the Gaelic League ensured that Irish became a compulsory subject on school curriculums and the first official language of Ireland.

There's no such thing as fairies
The burning of Bridget Cleary

On 15 March 1895, Bridget Cleary, the 28 year-old wife of Michael, a cooper, went missing from her home in Ballyvadlea, County Tipperary. Her husband claimed that she had been taken away by fairies and would return on a white horse. Days later her body was found in a shallow grave, having been burned to death.

In the days prior to her disappearance Bridget Cleary had taken a walk to deliver eggs. On her journey she passed the site of a fairy ring. She later became unwell. As time passed her condition became worse, and her husband Michael and her uncle Jack Dunne were convinced that Bridget had been taken by fairies and the woman in the bed was a changeling. In Irish folklore a fairy changeling was a duplicate put in the place of a real person, often a woman or child, after they were abducted by fairies. Michael was determined to drive out the changeling and get his wife back. On 13 March 1895, Michael

Kennedy and his mother, Mary Kennedy, went to visit Bridget. They found the house filled with people and witnessed a disturbing scene. Bridget was being held down by several men, including her husband Michael, her father and her brothers-in-law. They tried to force a concoction of herbs boiled in milk down her throat while shouting about witches and fairies. The following day Bridget told Michael she could see the police at the window, and he should leave her alone. Michael responded by

throwing the contents of a chamber pot over her.

The following day Bridget had disappeared. The story began to circulate that she was abducted by the fairies from the fairy ring she had so recently walked past.

What actually happened was so much more disturbing. Bridget was taken from her sickbed and brought to the kitchen which was once again filled with locals and family members. Michael Cleary prepared bread and jam and forced Bridget to eat. At first she complied but eventually refused to eat any more. Michael threw her to the ground, grabbed a hot stick from the fire, stripped her to her nightdress, doused her in lamp oil and set her alight. He told the onlookers that it was not his wife but a changeling and that Bridget would appear riding a white horse once the changeling was expelled. Nobody in the room tried to stop what was happening. When Bridget's charred remains were found in the shallow grave Michael Cleary and ten others were arrested for their part in her horrific murder. The charge against Cleary was dropped from murder to manslaughter. He was convicted and sentenced to 20 years in prison. Seven others were convicted of wounding Bridget; each received a sentence, ranging from six months to five years.

Knit one, purl one
The myth of the Aran jumper

Recognized by many as a symbol of Irish tradition, the Aran jumper got its name from the islands where the white patterned wool jumper originated. Despite its reputation as an emblem of Irishness the Aran jumper did not actually become a common item of clothing on island inhabitants until the 20th century.

The Aran Islands are a group of three islands, Inis Meain, Inis Oirr and the largest Inis Mór located off the west coast of Ireland. They are a *Gaeltacht* region, meaning that Irish is the predominant language. In the not too distant past, when stormy sea conditions prevailed the islands were completely cut off from the mainland without electricity, phone-lines, food, medical supplies or mail. Nowadays it is the islands' remoteness at the edge of the Atlantic Ocean that is one of Aran's most alluring characteristics, making the islands a popular destination for tourists looking to experience a quieter pace of life.

Despite their isolated location at the edge of Europe, the islands have been inhabited since approximately 3000 BC and are home to a wealth of ancient remains. Megalithic tombs provide definitive evidence of stone-age settlers; wedge tombs, similar to those found in the Burren, County Clare are found on all three islands. World Heritage site *Dún Aonghasa*, a spectacular stone fort, is perched on a dramatic 91 metre (300 foot) cliff edge location. Stone walls, thatched cottages and fisherman's boats and currachs pepper the islands' landscape. The remoteness of the location coupled with this sense of history no doubt helped fuel the legend of the Aran jumper.

It is widely believed that each family on the Aran Islands has a

Aran jumper

pattern that is exclusive to their family or *clan*. Folklore has it that the reason for this was because men on the island were predominantly fishermen. This was a dangerous profession on islands like those off the coast of the West of Ireland and many lost their lives at sea. The legend persists that the family pattern meant that a fisherman's body would be easily identifiable by his peers, should tragedy strike. This romantic folklore may have gained legs as a result of JM Synge's play *Riders to the Sea*, in which a drowning victim is identified by the stitches on his woollen jumper.

In the 1890s, encouraged by the Congested Districts Board, as a means of making money, the women of the Aran Islands began knitting socks to sell to the mainland. This later grew to include jumpers and the mythical Aran jumper was born. The women did not devise individual patterns or 'clan' styles so lost relatives could be easily identifiable but they did create unique and imaginative designs that gained in popularity as the 20th century progressed. They may have based their designs on jumpers worn by fishermen from the Channel Islands such as Guernsey, hence the Gaelicised word for jumper *geansaí*. Throughout the Channel Islands this type of jumper is often referred to as a gansey and they were normally blue in colour.

The first time the Aran jumper was offered for sale outside the Aran Islands was in the early 1930s. Perhaps one of Ireland's pioneering marketers, Muriel Gahan, the founder of Country Workers Ltd

and the Irish Homespun Society, offered Aran women money for their patterned jumpers and helped them to hone their craft. She sold thousands of jumpers to tourists from all over the world from her premises on Dublin's St Stephen's Green. As the jumper grew in popularity, appearing on the cover of *Vogue* magazine and the catwalks of Paris and Milan, so did its mythical status as a piece of clothing imbued with folklore and tradition.

WITH THIS RING, I THEE WED

Let love and friendship reign; the motto behind Ireland's most enduring piece of jewellery – the Claddagh ring. The ring consists of two hands encircled, holding a crowned heart. It is first thought to have appeared over 200 years ago but the story of how it came about, like many things in Ireland, is shrouded in myth and legend. It gets its name from a fishing village where it is thought to have originated.

How one wears their Claddagh

ring can reveal a lot to those in the know. If you are married the ring should be worn on your left hand with the heart pointing towards your heart. If you are single, wear it on your right hand with the heart pointing out, indicating that you are open to love!

Leave your jewels and gold wands in the bank and buy a revolver
Countess Markievicz

Born in London to the prominent Anglo-Irish Gore-Booth family of Lissadell, County Sligo, Constance Gore-Booth (1868–1927) was the eldest of five children. At nineteen years of age Constance was presented to Queen Victoria before embarking on a grand tour of Europe. When she returned she attended Art College in London. This experience opened her mind to ideas around women's suffrage, the labour movement and Irish nationalism. Constance married Casimir Dunin-Markievicz in 1900, giving birth to one

daughter, Maeve the following year.

In 1903 Markievicz moved to Dublin where she joined *Inghinidhe na hÉireann*, (Daughters of Ireland), a nationalist women's group, and in 1909 she co-founded *Na Fianna Éireann*, a nationalist youth movement with Bulmer Hobson. In 1911 she was arrested for demonstrating against King George V's visit to Ireland. In 1913–14 she provided food for workers and their families during the 1913 Lockout, a labour dispute in which thousands of people were locked out of their workplaces for refusing to reject union membership. Markievicz was a key player in the 1916 Easter Rising. She was appointed second in command to Michael Mallin (1874–1916) at St Stephen's Green. Upon surrendering she kissed her revolver before handing it over to the arresting British officer.

Markievicz was the only female who participated in the Rising to be court-martialled. The only reason she escaped assassination was because she was a woman. Sixteen of her peers and fellow combatants were executed. Joseph Plunkett,

Countess Markievicz

Edward Daly, Michael O'Hanrahan, Willie Pearse, John McBride, Eamonn Ceantt, Michael Mallin, Sean Heuston, Pádraic Pearse, Thomas Calrke, Thomas MacDonagh, Con Colbert, Sean MacDiarmada and James Connolly were all killed by firing squad at Kilaminham Gaol. Thomas Kent was shot at Cork Detention Barracks (now Collins Barracks). Roger Casement, as an Englishman, was hung for treason in Pentonville Prison in London.

The following year, under a general amnesty, Markievicz was released from prison. She became the first woman to be elected to the House of Commons although she refused to take her seat as she would not pledge allegiance to the British Crown. Instead, under the leadership of Eamon de Valera, the Irish Republicans set up their own provisional government, Dáil Éireann. Markievicz served as the Minister of Labour, from 1919 until she was defeated in the 1922 elections. That same year the Irish Free State was established. Markievicz was elected to the Dáil in the 1923 general election but, along with the other members of Sinn Féin, she once again refused to swear allegiance to the crown and did not take her seat. When Eamon de Valera founded the Fianna Fáil party in 1926 Markievicz joined and was again elected to the Dáil. She died a month later on 15 July 1927 without having taken her seat. She was refused a state funeral by the Irish Free State. She is buried in the Republican plot in Dublin's Glasnevin Cemetery.

DAUGHTERS OF IRELAND
**Founded by Maud Gonne
(1866–1953) in 1900, Inghinidhe
na hÉireann *was a radical Irish
nationalist women's organization.
The group adopted St Brigid as
their patron. The aims of the
organization were to achieve a fully
independent Ireland and to
encourage pursuit of the Irish
language and Irish customs in a
bid to combat the influence of
British newspapers. The pioneering
group were responsible for Ireland's
first ever nationalist-feminist
journal,* Bean na hÉireann**.

In April 1914 when **Cumann
na mBan** *was founded in Wynn's
Hotel in Dublin to work alongside
their male counterparts, the Irish
Volunteers in pursuit of an
independent Ireland,* **Inghinidhe
na hÉireann** *became a branch of*
**Cumann na mBan, Inghinidhe
na hÉireann** *had succeeded in
politicizing a generation of young
Irish women who would play a
pivotal role in the fight for
independence from Britain and
suffrage for all.*

But one man loved the pilgrim soul in you...
W.B. Yeats: a story of unrequited love

William Butler Yeats (1865–1939) was a leading light in the cultural and literary revival that took place in Ireland towards the end of the 19th century and beginning of the 20th century. This movement was important in restoring a sense of pride in being Irish among the people of Ireland. Unlike the Gaelic revival that was happening alongside this movement Yeats was not concerned with the Irish language. Born into a wealthy Anglo-Irish Protestant family he grew up in Dublin and later moved to London where he met John O'Leary and Standish O'Grady who introduced him to ancient Irish legends and folklore. This education had a profound effect on his work and how he wanted to affect change in Ireland. In 1902 he wrote *Cathleen Ní Houlihán* a play about Ireland and the willingness of young men to die for her. Following the horror of the 1916

W.B. Yeats

Easter Rising, Yeats was concerned that his words had encouraged Ireland's young men to do just that.

Something else that hugely influenced the poet's work was unrequited love. Throughout his life Yeats was infatuated, almost to the point of obsession, with Maud Gonne. The daughter of a British Captain, Gonne and Yeats met for the first time in his family home in London. She was well-travelled, well-educated and passionately dedicated to the cause of Irish nationalism. Yeats proposed to her several times throughout their lives but she always refused. They did eventually have a sexual relationship but it was short-lived. Despite this Yeats proposed to Maud Gonne's daughter Iseult in 1916 and again the following year. Like her mother before her Iseult also turned Yeats down. He was thirty years her senior.

In the end it was their political differences that divided Yeats and Gonne. Following the War of Independence Yeats supported the Free State government and Maud Gonne the anti-Treaty side. Despite his obsessive fascination with another woman, Yeats married Georgie Hyde-Lees on 20 October 1917. She was only three years older than Maud Gonne's daughter. He did not invite any family or friends to the London wedding. They had two children but Yeats was consistently unfaithful even after he became impotent. In a bid to rectify his impotence Yeats had a Steinach operation, a type of vasectomy which was believed to increase sexual vigour in men. Although Yeats maintained the procedure worked, it is believed he could no longer engage in full sexual intercourse. This however did not stop him from having affairs and when he died in France in 1939 both his lover, the journalist Edith Shackleton-Heal, and his wife Georgie were present.

THE NOBEL PRIZE FOR LITERATURE
In 1923 W.B. Yeats became the first Irish man to be awarded the **Nobel Prize in Literature** *'for his* **always inspired poetry, which in a highly artistic form gives expression to the spirit of a whole nation'.** *His place as one of the foremost figures in literature was well and truly cemented. Two years later George Bernard Shaw was also awarded the coveted prize. Both men would go on to fight against tightening censorship laws enforced by the Irish Free State. Samuel Beckett who was forced to leave Ireland because of these same strict laws was awarded the prize*

SOS *Titanic* calling
Harland & Wolff and The RMS Titanic

In the early hours of 15 April, 1912, the luxury passenger ship, the *RMS Titanic* sank after colliding into an iceberg off the coast of Newfoundland in the North Atlantic Sea. More than 1,500 passengers and crew lost their lives.

The story of the ill-fated liner began in the Belfast shipyard Harland and Wolff. By the early 1900s, Belfast was a thriving industrial city with a population of around 390,000. Many of its citizens were employed in the shipbuilding industries. The growth of the travel industry whether for first-class passengers wishing to see the world or third-class passengers searching for a better life, meant

Belfast

that there was a growing need for bigger and better passenger ships. In 1861, the Harland and Wolff yards covered an area of 1.5 acres and employed 100 men. The growth of the shipbuilding industry saw this increase to 10,000 men working out of an 80 acre space by 1897.

The *RMS Titanic* was conceived by J. Bruce Ismay, chief executive of White Star Line and William J. Pirrie chairman of Harland and Wolff to compete with Cunard, White Star's rivals in the passenger ship market. In 1907 Cunard launched the *Mauretania* and later that year, the magnificent *Lusitania* took to the seas. Tragically, the *Lusitania* was torpedoed off the South of Ireland by a German U-boat in 1915 resulting in the deaths of almost 1,200 people. The *Mauretania* remained in service until 1934. These ships were lauded the world over for their size and speed. That same year White Star commissioned three sister ships to vie with Cunard's luxury liners. The three sister ships, The *Olympic,* The *Titanic* and The *Britannic* (originally called the *Gigantic* but renamed

following *Titanic's* sinking) would measure 268 metres (882 feet) in length and 28 metres (92.5 feet) at their broadest point, making them the largest ships in the world.

In March 1909 work began on the *Titanic* at Harland and Wolff. Thomas Andrews from County Down was the chief designer of *Titanic.* Two years after construction began the enormous hull of the ship was released into the River Lagan. Over 100,000 people turned up to watch the launch giving some indication of the immense interest in these world class ships. The hull contained over 2,000 portholes from where *Titanic's* first-class passengers could see the ocean as

RMS Titanic *ready for launch*

Titanic sailed. The hull was moved to a fitting-out dock and it is here where the decks and luxurious fixtures and fittings were added to the luxury liner. These included facilities never before seen on a ship such as a swimming pool, squash courts and Turkish baths. The gym even included a mechanised horse! Almost a year later on 1 April 1912 *Titanic* was complete and ready to leave Belfast. A strong north-west wind delayed the departure by a day.

On 10 April 1912, *Titanic* began her maiden voyage from Southampton to Cherbourg, France, among huge fanfare. She picked up passengers in Cherbourg then headed for her last stop in Cobh, County Cork. From Cobh she set sail on that fateful voyage towards New York.

TITANIC'S *FIRST VICTIM*

1,500 people lost their lives aboard the **Titanic***, but the ill-fated luxury liner was responsible for the lives of some unfortunate people who died during the ship's construction. Fifteen-year-old Samuel Joseph Scott fell from a ladder, sustaining a fatal skull fracture two years before* **Titanic** *set sail. Samuel Scott was one of 15,000 workers involved in assembling the massive ship and is believed to be one of approximately twelve people who died during its construction. It was the job of the young boy and others like him to carry scorching metal rivets with a pair of tongs from the furnace where they were heated to the holes into which they fitted. The rivets were then hammered into place and allowed to cool, tightly cinching* **Titanic's** *steel frame together.*

Samuel Scott had lain in an unmarked grave in Belfast City Cemetery but following the publication of a fictionalized account of Samuel's journey as a ghost on the **Titanic***, by children's* *writer Nicola Pierce, the teenage boy's final resting place was marked with a headstone in Belfast City Cemetery in 2011, almost 100 years after his untimely death.*

We declare the right of the people of Ireland to the ownership of Ireland...
The 1916 Proclamation

With the British government's attention concerned with The Great War, a group of disillusioned men and women came together with the aim of creating an independent Irish Republic. Easter Sunday 23 April 1916 was fixed as the date for the Rising. Having enlisted help from German volunteers to obtain arms, a ship called the *Aud* set sail for the coast of Kerry. However on Good Friday, thanks to Russian intelligence the *Aud* was intercepted. Rather than let the arms fall to the English the ship was scuttled and its cargo of 20,000 rifles and a million rounds of ammunition were lost. Roger Casement (1864–1916) who had been charged with responsibility for the weapons arrived by U-Boat but was caught, arrested and brought to Dublin where as a British citizen he was tried for treason. The planned uprising was not off to a good start.

Despite the lack of munitions, volunteers throughout the country had received news to continue with plans to carry out military manoeuvres and parades on Easter Sunday. When Eoin MacNeill, the commander-in-chief of the Irish Volunteers, learned that despite having no weapons or ammunition the Irish Republican Brotherhood (IRB) and the Irish Citizen Army actually intended to go ahead with the planned uprising, he was incredulous. MacNeill immediately inserted an advertisement in the *Sunday Independent* cancelling all Easter Sunday mobilization activities. This caused much confusion among the Volunteers. The leaders held an emergency meeting at Liberty Hall on Sunday morning and decided to go ahead with the uprising the following day. At noon on Easter Monday a

Crowds outside The GPO

company of a few hundred Irish Volunteers and Irish Citizen Army, led by James Connolly (1868–1916), Patrick Pearse (1879–1916), Joseph Plunkett (1887–1916), Seán MacDiarmada (1883–1916) and Tom Clarke (1858–1916), marched from Liberty Hall to Sackville Street, (now O'Connell Street), and occupied the General Post Office (GPO) in the centre of Dublin city.

At 12.45pm after raising a tri-colour from a flagpole and a green banner with the words *'Irish Republic'* written on it, Patrick Pearse, the commander-in-chief of the insurgent army stepped outside the GPO and read aloud the *'Proclamation of the Irish Republic'*.

The Proclamation was drafted and signed by seven of the Rising leaders acting as the Provisional Government: Thomas J. Clarke, Seán Mac Diarmada, Thomas MacDonagh (1878–1916), Patrick Pearse, Éamonn Ceannt (1881–916), James Connolly and Joseph Plunkett. These men became known as the seven signatories. The Proclamation was printed by Christopher Brady who was the printer for James Connolly's (leader of the Citizen Army) newspaper the *Workers Republic.* From 8.30pm on Easter Sunday until after midday on Easter Monday, 2,500 copies of the Proclamation were printed for distribution around Dublin city. Although it is believed that Patrick Pearse was responsible for drafting the document, the socialist viewpoint of James Connolly in particular is evident in the sentiments expressed in the Proclamation. It promised an Ireland that embraced inclusion and social justice for all citizens including men, women and children. Ultimately the Rising failed but those who had fought for an Independent Ireland had begun a battle that would eventually result in Ireland gaining partial independence from the United Kingdom.

THE PEN IS MIGHTIER THAN THE SWORD

Michael Joseph O'Rahilly (1875–1916), known commonly as The O'Rahilly was an Irish republican and nationalist and a founding member of the Irish Volunteers. Like his comrade Eoin MacNeill, he opposed the actions that took part on Easter Monday. This however, did not stop him from taking part. Having spent the weekend travelling to Limerick and back alerting other would-be insurgents that the Rising was called off, he arrived home to learn that it was actually just about to begin!

He fought with the GPO garrison throughout Easter Week. On Friday 28 April 1916, one day before the revolutionaries surrendered, with the GPO on fire, O'Rahilly volunteered to lead a party of men away from the building and along a route to Williams and Woods, a factory on Great Britain Street (now Parnell Street). They were intercepted by British machine gun fire and O'Rahilly was shot. He slumped in a doorway on Moore Street, wounded and bleeding badly. He managed to run across the road, finding shelter in Sackville Lane (now O'Rahilly Parade). In his pocket was a letter from his son. On the back of it he penned one last letter to his wife.

The letter has been inscribed on a lime and bronze memorial plaque by artist Shane Cullen. It is mounted on a wall on O'Rahilly Parade. It reads:

'Written after I was shot. Darling Nancy I was shot leading a rush up Moore Street and took refuge in a doorway. While I was there I heard the men pointing out where I was and made a bolt for the laneway I am in now. I got more than one bullet I think. Tons and tons of love dearie to you and the

**boys and to Nell and Anna.
It was a good fight anyhow.
Please deliver this to Nannie
O' Rahilly, 40 Herbert Park,
Dublin. Goodbye Darling.'**

Down with this sort of thing!
The censorship of Ireland's literary elite

Sean O'Casey, George Bernard Shaw and Samuel Beckett: renowned Irish writers, respected throughout the world for their contribution to literature, yet at the height of their careers they were actually banned in Ireland. Ireland was a predominantly Catholic country. This fact strongly influenced the newly independent Irish Free State's decision to introduce stricter censorship laws. The *Censorship of Publications Act* was passed in 1929 and a Censorship of Publications Board was formed. The board's main function was to monitor all literature that arrived on Irish shores, from newspapers to works of fiction ensuring that no

obscene literature could be read by the Irish population. Of huge concern was the quantity of newspapers and magazines from Britain that mentioned divorce and contraception. The Censorship Board believed such taboo subjects were not suitable for Irish audiences!

Although newspapers were the original target of the board, they soon set their sights on fiction and in 1930 Liam O'Flaherty's *The House of Gold* became the first book by an Irish writer to be banned in Ireland. From that moment on the number of fictionalized works being banned began to steadily increase. 1954 was a record year, with 1,034 prohibitions, six of which were books by Irish authors. The list of banned authors became a veritable 'Who's Who' of Irish literature. John McGahern, who would go on to write the internationally acclaimed *Amongst Women* actually lost his job as a teacher as a result of having his second novel *The Dark* banned. Edna O'Brien's novel *The Country Girls* was reportedly burned by the local parish priest. She spoke openly of the shame she felt and that she had brought upon her family after being banned.

In the 1960s, on the pages of Irish newspapers and magazines, calls for reform became more frequent and vehement. The perceived harsh treatment of John McGahern caused controversy in the Irish senate. This coupled with Edna O'Brien's vociferousness about her own banning and the affect that it had on her personal life, would eventually lead to the demise of the Censorship Board as it stood. In 1967 the Minister for Justice suggested an amendment to the Act meaning that if a book had been banned for twelve or more years, the ban would be automatically lifted. This resulted in over 5,000 banned books becoming immediately available for Irish audiences to read.

DON'T MENTION ULYSSES

Although James Joyce's modernist **magnum opus** *is often referred to as one of Ireland's banned books,* **Ulysses** *was actually never banned by the Irish Censorship Board. The* **Little Review,** *an American literary magazine, serialised Joyce's* **Ulysses** *from March 1918 until December 1920. Following the publication of a chapter which featured a scene considered 'indecent' by the US courts, the* **Little Review** *was forced to discontinue the serialization. The US ban was lifted in 1933 and the*

James Joyce

work was published in its entirety. No Irish bookseller was brave enough to openly import it for sale until the censorship laws were relaxed in the late 1960s.

The men of Ireland were hurling when the Gods of Greece were young
Hurling and Gaelic Football

Hurling is often described as the fastest field sport in the world. It is unique to Ireland and the skill, speed and agility required to play it have earned it a reputation as being one of the most exciting games in the world to watch. With Handball and Gaelic football, it is one of Ireland's national sports.

Hurling predates recorded history with the first known mention of the legendary sport recorded in the 12th century *Book of Leinster*. The writing refers to a game of hurling at the Battle of Moytura in 1272 BC between the legendary Tuatha Dé Danann and the Firbolgs, two rival tribes. The Brehon Laws allude to compensation for injuries sustained as a result of hurling. Later the Statutes of Kilkenny (1366) and Statutes of Galway expressly forbid members of the Anglo-Irish ruling classes to play the native Irish sport. Despite this the game flourished up until the 19th century. The detrimental effects of the Great Famine meant that the game was in danger of disappearing from the Irish landscape in favour of games from Britain. Despite this the skilful ball and stick sport was beginning to become popular with the landed gentry. They formed clubs throughout Dublin including one at Hurley Club Trinity College. The form of hurling they played was more similar in style to hockey than the more rambunctious sport played by farming and working classes. The same could not be said for Gaelic football. Its popularity was in decline with the upper classes as they embraced rugby and soccer. Gaelic Football was common throughout the middle ages in Ireland in the same way that soccer and rugby in some form or other grew in popularity

Hurl and Sliotar

throughout Europe. As with hurling there was a decline in the numbers playing the sport throughout the country following the Famine. Concerned for the future of these indigenous sports Michael Cusack (1847–1906), a teacher and sports enthusiast from North Clare set up the Dublin Hurling Club in direct opposition to Trinity's Hurley Club. Cusack began campaigning for a national organization that would promote Irish sports. In November 1884 at a meeting in Thurles, County Tipperary and with the support of Maurice Davin (1842–1927) the Gaelic Athletic Association (GAA) was formed and the future of these indigenous sports secured.

The GAA was unashamedly nationalist in its outlook forbidding its members from playing non-Gaelic games and banning members of the British Crown Forces. Its formation had the desired effect on the popularity of the sports and membership increased steadily. Today the GAA is the largest sporting organization in Ireland with clubs in every town in the country and cities throughout the world including New York, Sydney and Tokyo.

If you build it, they will come
The story of a stadium

Within a few weeks of the foundation of the Gaelic Athletic Association, Thomas Croke, the Roman Catholic Archbishop of Cashel, gave the organization his approval. In doing so he became the organization's first patron. In 1913 the GAA's main stadium was named in his honour. Originally a private sports ground known as Jones' Road Sports Stadium, in December 1908 Frank Dineen, a former GAA President and General Secretary, purchased the ground in trust for the use of the GAA for the sum of £3,250. Five years later the GAA purchased the grounds from Dineen for £3,500. The ground was then renamed Croke Memorial Park.

As the GAA took ownership of the sports ground, Ireland entered the revolutionary years. This is reflected in the history of the stadium. In the aftermath of the Easter Rising in 1916, rubble from bombed buildings on O'Connell Street was transported to Croke Park where it was used to make a stand for spectators at the north end of the sports ground. Although the stadium has changed beyond all recognition this viewing mound and the adjacent Nally Stand remain the only standing terraces in the stadium. It is called Hill 16 and has a particularly special place in the hearts of Dublin supporters. The stadium's darkest moment happened in 1920 at the height of the War of Independence when, on 21 November, British Troops entered the grounds and opened fire during a match between Tipperary and Dublin. Thirteen spectators and one Tipperary footballer, Michael Hogan, were killed on what became known as *'Bloody Sunday'*. The Hogan Stand, built in 1924 was named in the player's honour.

Throughout its history Croke Park has under-gone several renovations. In 1966 the lower Cusack Stand became a seated area reducing the capacity of the national stadium. Prior to this the highest attendance ever recorded at an All-Ireland Football Final was 90,556 at the 1961 Down vs Offaly final. The most dramatic changes to the stadium began in 1993 with the implementation of a rolled out redevelopment plan which began with the demolition and reconstruction of the Cusack Stand. Over a period of twelve years Croke Park was transformed into a world class stadium with a capacity of 82,300, making it one of the largest stadiums in Europe and the largest not to be used primarily for soccer.

Croke Park

RULE 42

Landsdowne Road Stadium was the official stadium of both the Irish soccer and rugby teams. In 2005 negotiations began with the GAA to allow these teams to temporarily use Croke Park as their home ground as Landsdowne Road Stadium was being demolished and replaced. Croke Park was the only stadium that could feasibly host the expected crowds. The GAA's Rule 42 prohibited the playing of non-Gaelic games at GAA venues and it appeared that they may not be willing to change the rules. However, following heated debate in the media, on 16 April 2005 GAA Congress voted to abolish Rule 42 and open Croke Park to other sports.

The following January it was announced that Croke Park would stage both Six Nations games and soccer internationals. On 24 February 2007 the Irish rugby team took to the Croke Park pitch to play England in the **Six Nations Championship.** *As* **God Save the Queen** *rang out*

across the stadium where almost a century earlier 'Bloody Sunday' had occurred it was a poignant reminder of how far Anglo-Irish relations had come and the uniting power of sport.

The Field
The National Ploughing Championships

On the 16 February 1931, forty farmers from nine counties around Ireland met in a twenty-six acre field in Athy, Co. Kildare to figure out which county had the best ploughmen in Ireland. The event was the result of an argument between two friends – one from Wexford, one from Kildare, over which county could plough the best. A challenge was laid down, word spread and several other counties came on board. It was to be the first ever official ploughing Championship in the world. Wexford won the trophy and the second Championships were held the following year in Gorey. Stricter rules were enforced and a '*national style'* of ploughing was introduced. The event was attended by over 3,000 spectators and reported on by local and national newspapers. It continued to grow and in 1939 despite the outbreak of World War II in Europe the Championships had their most successful year to date; both the number of spectators and competitors increased.

As the years went on the event diversified, introducing new competitions to appeal to a broader range of visitors. These included horse-shoeing competitions and sheaf-throwing. 1942 saw the introduction of the first ever National Tractor Ploughing Competition. There were seventeen participants. In 1946 President of Ireland Seán T. O'Kelly attended the Championships. Successive presidents have continued to attend

highlighting the importance of the Championship as both a cultural and economical phenomenon. Although originally conceived as a ploughing competition in which the main event is expert international ploughmen pitting their skills against one another, it is now also a massive trade show, and the largest outdoor event of its kind in Europe. Exhibitions vary from livestock and machinery to trade stalls, craft stalls, vintage motors, fashion shows, interior design and art exhibitions. It takes place over three days and is attended by nearly 300,000 visitors. New competitions have been added including the annual Brown Bread Baking competition, sheep-shearing, cow-milking and welly throwing. The event extends over 700 acres of field. Over the course of the event approximately 16,000 litres of milk and 60,000 cups of tea and coffee are consumed. In 2015 a Guinness World Record for most cups of teas poured in an hour was set – 1,848 cups!

Ploughing

Those magnificent men in their flying machines
Foynes: European terminal for transatlantic flights

For a brief moment in history, a small Irish town called Foynes was home to one of the largest civilian airports in Europe. Foynes location on the southern bank of the Shannon estuary with a sheltered harbour and railway connection to Limerick city and beyond meant it was the ideal location for a new European terminal for transatlantic flights. Pan-American Airlines commissioned Charles Lindbergh (1902–1974) to find a suitable base for their flying boat service from the United States to Ireland and Foynes became that place. On 9 July 1939, the Pan-Am owned *Yankee Clipper* landed at Foynes completing the first ever commercial passenger flight on a direct route between America and Europe. The flying boat could carry thirty-five passengers in sleeper accommodation. It had a dining room that could seat fourteen people for a seven-course meal. Two air stewards prepared and served the food. The flying boat had an observation deck and a private honeymoon suite to the rear. There was also sleeping quarters for the crew. Facilities like these ensured

A flying boat

travel by flying boat was the preserve of politicians, Hollywood stars and the extremely wealthy.

The Irish Free State elected to remain neutral during World War II so flying boats from England en route to Portugal and Africa flew via Foynes to avoid fighter planes over France. These flights normally arrived at Foynes at dawn and departed at sunset to avoid unnecessary public attention. Many of the passengers on transatlantic flights were actually allied military and diplomatic personal on active duty.

As well as military personnel, during its time as a transatlantic hub Foynes played host to many personalities including John F. Kennedy, Ernest Hemingway, Gracie Fields, Humphrey Bogart, First Lady Eleanor Roosevelt and Maureen O'Hara. In fact Maureen O'Hara was married to a renowned pilot, Charlie Blair. He was to fly the last scheduled flying boat from Foynes to New York in 1945. The following day, 24 October 1945, he returned to Ireland piloting an American

Airlines landplane at Rineanna, now Shannon Airport. The flight took eight and a half hours and signalled the beginning of a new chapter in aviation history. Foynes Airport closed the following year.

IRISH COFFEE

On a cold winter's night in 1943 the pilot of a flying boat on course from Foynes to New York decided to turn back until weather conditions improved. The Foynes control tower received a Morse Code message that staff were to return to the terminal to prepare food and drinks for the staff and passengers. Joe Sheridan, the head chef from County Tyrone decided to add a measure of whiskey to cups of hot coffee, topped with cream for the cold travellers.
Local legend tells that one passenger asked if Joe had used Brazilian coffee in the hot drink and the barman jokingly responded, 'No, it's Irish coffee'. A

few weeks later Joe prepared the hot liqueur in a stemmed glass and the Irish coffee as we know it was born. Joe Sheridan later moved to San Francisco to work at the Buena Vista Cafe where journalist Stanton Delaplane of the **San Francisco Chronicle** *had brought back the secret recipe from Ireland. Today the Buena Vista Cafe is renowned for its Irish coffee, serving up to 2,000 Irish coffees a day.*

She was lovely and fair like the rose of the summer
The Rose of Tralee

In the late 1950s the town of Tralee in County Kerry was like many other towns around Ireland: suffering as a result of economic depression and mass unemployment. In a bid to create a buzz around the town the previously successful Carnival Queen competition was reintroduced.

It proved successful and over a pint in Roger Harty's pub in Tralee a group of locals led by Dan Nolan, publisher of *The Kerryman* newspaper, came up with the idea of extending the Carnival Queen concept and so the Rose of Tralee festival was born.

The original idea for the festival was for five women to compete for the title of Rose of Tralee. The women came from New York, London, Birmingham, Dublin and Kerry; all towns synonymous with Irish diaspora. The criteria for entering was that the women had to be unmarried and have parents from Tralee. Dan Nolan travelled to the United States where he received promises of support from the New York mayor. The first festival was a huge success with over 150 people travelling from New York to Tralee. The State solicitor even provided mock Kerry Passports that were stamped for the returning ex-pats when they entered the kingdom of Kerry. In the summer of 1959 Alice O'Sullivan from Dublin became the first ever Rose of Tralee and an Irish institution was born. The following year the selection criteria for the festival was expanded to include women whose parents came from Kerry and in 1967 this was extended further to include any women of Irish ancestry.

The festival now attracts would-be Roses from Birmingham, Boston, Darwin, Dubai, France, London, Luxembourg, Newcastle, New York, New Orleans, New Zealand, Perth, Queensland, San Francisco, Southern California, South Australia, Sydney, Texas and Toronto to name but a few. In 1964 Margaret O'Keefe became the only woman from Tralee to have ever won the contest. Despite the fact that the competition has been labelled as out-dated it continues to draw crowds of tourists to Tralee every August. It is on National Television over two nights and almost 700,000 viewers tune in to watch the Roses take to the stage to talk about their lives and links to Ireland. The competition has been

presented by some of Ireland's top broadcasters including Gay Byrne, Ryan Tubridy, Ray D'Arcy and Terry Wogan. Kathleen Watkins remains the only female to have presented the show. The organizers claim it is not a beauty pageant and that the winner is picked by a committee based on the woman's *'aspirations, ambitions, intellect, social responsibility and Irish heritage'*. To prove that it is moving with the times organizers amended the rules in 2007 to include married women and the following year unmarried mothers were allowed to compete for the first time for the coveted title of Rose of Tralee.

The case for humanity
The death penalty in Ireland

It was not until 1990 that the Irish government passed the Criminal Justice Act, prohibiting capital punishment in Ireland for all crimes, including treason and capital murder. These offences were now punishable by a mandatory 40-year jail term without parole. In 2001, following a referendum, a constitutional ban on the death penalty, even during wartime was passed. Although a ban was not in place, the last Irish person to die by hanging was Michael Manning in 1954.

Manning was sentenced to death by a jury following his trial for murder. Catherine Cooper, a nurse, was badly beaten and sexually assaulted by Manning before she died of suffocation. A petition to have Manning's sentence commuted to life imprisonment was signed by the family of the victim but the authorities paid no attention. Manning himself wrote to the Minister for Justice seeking clemency but his pleas were ignored.

Albert Pierrepoint (1905–1992) arrived from London to carry out the hanging. In the early 1940s an attempt was made to recruit a local executioner and a man known by the pseudonym of Thomas Johnston was sent to Pierrepoint for training. Johnston was supposed to carry out the hanging of Joseph McManus in 1947 but was unable to go through with the act. Pierrepoint, who was there should his trainee need assistance, had to take over. Rather than recruit again, the government continued to call on Pierrepoint's expertise. On the morning of his execution Manning read the *Irish Independent*, smoked cigarettes and attended mass.

Although others after Manning would be sentenced to death none were actually killed. One such criminal was Mamie Cadden. Originally from America, Cadden performed back-street abortions on hundreds of women in Dublin. In 1956 a patient, Helen O'Reilly died on her makeshift operating table. Cadden left Helen O'Reilly's body in the street. She was sentenced to hang before having her sentence commuted to life imprisonment. One year later she was declared insane and moved to Dundrum Mental Hospital. She died there two years later.

Countess Markievicz was sentenced to death for her part in the Easter Rising, but was recommended for mercy for the sole reason that she was a woman. Markievicz was one of a large number of women who had the ultimate punishment imposed on them in 20th-century Ireland only to have the sentence commuted to imprisonment at the last minute. In 1964 Irish law was altered so that the death sentence could only be pronounced in the case of capital, or political murder. However, following Manning's hanging in 1954, no man or woman was killed as a result of the death penalty in Ireland.

The Taking of Christ
The lost Caravaggio

For 30 years, there hung a painting *The Betrayal of Christ* on the dining room wall of the Leeson Street Jesuit Community. It was accredited to Gabriel Von Honthorst (1592–1660), a Dutch painter renowned for painting in the style of Michelangelo Merisi da Caravaggio (1571–1610). In 1990 Fr Noel Barber was commissioned to renovate the Jesuit house. Fr

Barber employed Sergio Benedetti, an Italian conservator at the National Gallery of Ireland (NGI) to restore the painting as part of the overall work on the house. The NGI agreed on the grounds that it was in fact a Honthorst in return for which the Jesuits would make the painting available to the NGI for exhibition. On seeing the painting in the dining room of the Jesuit house, Benedetti thought the painting was the best copy of a lost Caravaggio – if not a lost Caravaggio. Eighteen months of restoration, tests and an inquiry into the provenance of the painting established that it was the 'lost' Caravaggio.

Originally commissioned for the Roman Marquis Ciriaco Mattei at the end of the 18th century it had been bought by Scottish art collector William Hamilton Nisbet in the early 19th century. In 1921, Marie Monica Lea-Wilson from Gorey in County Wexford bought a religious painting accredited to Honthorst in an estate sale in Edinburgh. Dr Lea-Wilson gave the painting as a gift to Fr Thomas

National Gallery of Ireland

Finlay, a friend and Jesuit priest. It was to hang in the dining room for thirty years while the Jesuits went about their daily lives, a treasure of the art world waiting to be discovered.

After *The Betrayal of Christ* was cleaned, and following painstaking research led by Benedetti, the painting was revealed, to an astounded art world, to be the 'lost' Caravaggio entitled *The Taking of Christ*. It was given to the Irish State on 'indefinite loan' by the Jesuits and unveiled to the public in the National Gallery of Ireland in 1993. Unfortunately Dr Lea-Wilson died in 1971 two decades before the 'lost' Caravaggio was revealed.

TO YOU I BESTOW

In his last will and testament, George Bernard Shaw (1856–1950) bequeathed one third of his posthumous royalties to the National Gallery of Ireland. Bernard Shaw left school at fourteen years of age and claimed the Gallery was 'the place to which I owe much of the only real education I ever got as a boy in Eire.' *The popularity of his play* Pygmalion *and its later adaptation to the big screen as* My Fair Lady, *meant that the Gallery received substantial royalties. This in turn improved the Gallery's ability to purchase paintings allowing it to compete with its European counterparts. A life-size bronze statue of the playwright stands proudly inside the entrance to the Gallery and a wing has been named in honour of his generosity.

'Ladies and Gentlemen, to whom it concerns, it's *The Late Late Show...*'

The world's longest-running chat show

From inauspicious beginnings as a summer 'filler' show on Ireland's national broadcaster *Teilifís Éireann*, *The Late Late Show* is the longest-running chat show in the world. The idea for the show was conceived by producer Tom McGrath, who had worked in Canada and hoped to create an Irish version of the American chat show *The Tonight Show.* Presented by Gay Byrne, a disc jockey, newsreader and continuity announcer, the first show was broadcast at 11.20pm on 6 July 1962. Count Cyril McCormack, Ken Gray, George Desmond Hodnett and Harry Thuillier were the show's first guests. Despite its late start time and uninspiring lineup the host's easy manner appealed to Irish audiences and the following winter *Teilifís Éireann* gave Gay Byrne the covetable Saturday night slot. When Gay Byrne took up the job as host of *The Late Late Show* he was also holding down a position at the BBC. He was contracted to present a Saturday afternoon show called *Open House* meaning he was not always available to return to Ireland for the Saturday night chat show. Because of this, Frank Hall took on the mantle in 1964 but proved unpopular with audiences. Byrne returned the following year only missing a handful of shows due to illness until his retirement in 1999. On his final show he was presented with a Harley Davidson by Bono and Larry Mullen of U2 fame. Pat Kenny went on to present the show for ten years until Ryan Tubridy took over in 2009. Byrne presented the show for thirty-seven years and was key to its longevity, often chairing frank and open debates amongst panellists and audience members on contentious subjects.

The Late Late Show was at its height as topics including contraception, divorce, homosexuality and the relevance of the Irish language were openly debated in Ireland for the first time. The live format added an element of excitement to the show. In 1966 excitement levels were peaked when during a telephone quiz, a viewer revealed she had not worn any clothes to bed on her wedding night. The following morning the Bishop of Clonfert denounced the show for encouraging loose morals. The controversy carried into the weekly papers and was dubbed *'the case of the Bishop and the Nightie'*.

Although primarily a show for adults, in the 1970s producers introduced a one-off half-hour slot to help parents struggling with Christmas gift ideas for children. This soon became an annual special in which children were the stars of the show, testing toys and performing on stage. While the show's relevance as a forum for public debate may have waned *The Toy Show* has become an institution drawing in more Irish viewers than any other television show.

Who stole the horse?
The kidnapping of Shergar

In the early 1980s Shergar was undoubtedly the most famous horse in the world. At three years of age the bay colt with a distinctive white blaze on its face and four white 'socks' won the 1981 Derby by ten lengths, a record distance for Britain's biggest flat race. He had similar successes at the Irish and King George Derby winning the hearts of horse-lovers the world over. Owned by the Aga Khan there were fears he would be sent to an American stud farm once he retired but the horse was returned to his birthplace of Ireland. He was syndicated for stud for £10,000,000 – forty shares worth £250,000 each, six of which were kept by the Aga Khan. In his first season owners paid up to £80,000 for the privilege of having a colt or filly by Shergar. It was expected he would cover in the region of fifty-five mares until one of the strangest kidnappings in Irish history took place.

Shortly after 8.30pm on 8 February 1983, Jim Fitzgerald, the

head-groom at Ballymany stud, heard a knock on his door. Three masked and armed men barged their way in and demanded a £2,000,000 ransom for Shergar. The horse was loaded into a stolen horsebox and whisked away never to be seen again. The kidnappers had chosen the day before Ireland's major racehorse sale to abduct the prize stud. Horseboxes were being driven up and down the country making it more difficult for the stallion to be found.

Speculation grew over who on earth would kidnap a horse. The *Garda Síochána* began a painstaking search, asking the public to check all stables, sheds and barns in a bid to locate the missing colt. It was the height of the Troubles in Northern Ireland and suspicion soon fell on the IRA. Finally, a call came into the BBC newsroom in Belfast from an anonymous caller asking for three horse-racing journalists from London to meet the following day at Belfast's Europa Hotel. Journalists and photographers thronged to Ireland as the world waited to see if Shergar would be returned. A series of phone calls ended with the message that there had been an accident and Shergar was dead. No-one has ever admitted the theft of Shergar and the body of the horse has never been found. The most valuable horse in the world disappeared without a trace.

THE EUROPA HOTEL

The Europa Hotel is a testament to the hope and resilience of Belfast and its citizens. Between 1970 and 1994, the hotel was damaged by explosions thirty-three times, gaining it the disquieting title of the most bombed hotel in the world. Opening its doors during the summer of 1971, the Europa was where the press and politicians gathered in Belfast as the Troubles escalated. A permanent notice was attached to the bedroom doors warning that due to the civil unrest in Belfast, guests may have to speedily evacuate the building. In the summer of 1973, **The Irish Times** *office moved into the Europa Hotel after their Belfast premises on Great Victoria Street was destroyed by a car bomb. The Europa became an obvious target for the IRA because of its location, visibility and the people who stayed and met there. When the peace process began a sense of optimism surrounded the hotel. Guests including Bill and Hilary Clinton, Bob Dylan, Brad Pitt and Julia Roberts stayed there. The Europa announced its support for the Good Friday Agreement by unfurling a large banner from the top of the hotel. It said one word: YES.*

I did it the Wild Atlantic Way
Ireland's west coast touring route

The Wild Atlantic Way is a scenic coastal route encompassing nine counties and 1,553 miles (2,500 km) on Ireland's west coast. Previously it was a series of roads, tracks, beaches and towns but in 2013 *Fáilte Ireland* packaged the entire coastal route from Donegal to Cork as a touring route with excellent signage, creating one of Ireland's most popular tourist attractions.

The Wild Atlantic Way stretches from the Inishowen Peninsula in County Donegal to Kinsale in West Cork. It encompasses some of Ireland's most popular and enduring visitor attractions but also allows visitors to follow a series of looped itineraries and discover the road less travelled, taking in spectacular beaches in Sligo or leafy walks in Leitrim.

The Cliffs of Moher in County Clare are Ireland's most visited natural attraction. They get their name from a ruined headland fort or *mohor* in Gaelic which was demolished in the early 1800s to make way for a signal tower during the Napoleonic wars. On a clear day visitors can see as far as the Dingle Peninsula in Kerry and the Maumturk Mountains in Connemara. Perhaps not quite as well known but equally as impressive are the Sliabh Liag cliffs in County Donegal. Reaching a height of 601 metres (1,971 feet) these magnificent cliffs soar almost three times the height of the Cliffs of Moher making them Europe's highest accessible seacliffs.

Although the west coast's changeable climate may not encourage visitors in for a paddle in the Atlantic Ocean, the gusty winds and rolling waves have earned Ireland a reputation as one of Europe's top surfing spots. Places such as Dunfanaghy and Bundoran in Donegal, Strandhill in Sligo, Lahinch in Clare and Ballybunion in Kerry offer surfers of all levels a taste of what it's like to surf the Atlantic Ocean without going State-side.

Other natural wonders on Ireland's magnificent Wild Atlantic

The Cliffs of Moher

Way include the 320 million year old sea pools known as Pollock Holes in Kilkee, County Clare. The reef containing the natural sea pools are known as Pollock Holes as they contain small pollock, a type of fish, for part of the year. The main pools range in depth from one metre (3.28 feet) to 2.5 metre (8.2 feet) deep and vary in size from approximately 50 metres (164 feet) long to 20 metres (65 feet) wide and act as excellent swimming pools at low tide. At one point the Pollock Hole closest to the Kilkee shore was for female bathers only, while the farthest one was for men.

ALIVE AND FLIPPING

Fungi the Dolphin arrived on the shores of Dingle, County Kerry in 1983 and achieved 'permanent' resident status in 1984 having consistently escorted the local fishermen's boats in and out of Dingle harbour. The playful dolphin has been delighting visitors to the Kerry Coast ever since. As the years progressed and Fungi remained in the waters around Dingle, scepticism grew that it was actually more than one dolphin. There have even been rumours that there is a mechanised dolphin swimming and frolicking in the Kerry waters. Fungi's characteristic dorsal fin signifies that it is actually the same dolphin that has been swimming alongside the boats of Dingle since 1983. A bronze statue of the town's most famous inhabitant has been erected in the harbour.

Yes Equality!
The vote for marriage equality in Ireland

On Saturday 23 May 2015 Ireland made history by becoming the first country in the world to legalise same-sex marriage by popular vote. Voters went to the polls the day before with the results being announced at an historic event in the courtyard at Dublin Castle the following day. Early indications pointed towards a majority yes vote and in the end a whopping 62 per cent of the Irish Republic's electorate voted in favour of equality marriage. Only one of the forty-three constituencies returned a no vote. The turnout was high with 60.5 per cent of the electorate placing a vote. This put the marriage equality

referendum in the top five of referendums held in Ireland. The highest turnout in any referendum was for the 1975 question on joining the European Economic Community when over 70 per cent of the electorate cast their ballot.

Since 2010 same-sex couples could obtain a civil partnership. This offered similar legal protection to married couples in areas such as property, tax, social welfare, immigration and pensions. However, these legal protections could be amended by an Act of the government. In order for same-sex couples to be afforded actual equality a change had to be made to the wording of the Irish constitution. For this to happen, a referendum had to be held.

The Offences Against the Persons Act, 1861 had criminalized male homosexuality in both Ireland and Britain. This Act was abolished in the United Kingdom in 1967 but it was not until 1993 that *Dáil Éireann* passed a Bill decriminalizing homosexuality in Ireland. This was a result of a ruling by the European Court of

Human Rights that Ireland's anti-gay laws contravened the European Convention on Human Rights. David Norris (1944–), a key player in the Gay Rights Movement in Ireland, was fundamental to these changes coming about. Norris had campaigned tirelessly throughout the 1970s and 1980s for the decriminalization of homosexuality. He helped found the Irish Gay Rights Movement and took a legal challenge against the State. He was defeated in both the High Court and the Supreme Court. In the Supreme Court in 1983 he was represented by a future President of Ireland and Human Rights campaigner, Mary Robinson. Norris's success at European Court level opened the way for the subsequent decriminalization of homosexuality in 1993 and the eventual legalization of same-sex marriage twenty-two years later. Having fought tirelessly for equal rights for same-sex couples David Norris was received to rapturous applause in the courtyard of Dublin Castle on the afternoon of 23 May 2015.

WE ARE ALL IN THE GUTTER, BUT SOME OF US ARE LOOKING AT THE STARS
Dublin born Oscar Wilde (1854–1900) is revered the world over for his intellect and wit. His novel, **The Picture of Dorian Gray** **is regarded as a classic and** **The Importance of Being Earnest,** **Wilde's most famous play, is still performed in theatres today, yet the**

Oscar Wilde

*much-loved flamboyant playwright
and novelist died in poverty at the
age of 46. Wilde was arrested for
having a homosexual relationship
and imprisoned for two years on
charges of 'gross indecency'. On
release from prison he fled to Paris
where he died three years later.
Witty to the end his last words
were 'My wallpaper and I are
fighting a duel to the death. One or
the other of us has to go'.*

Like a bridge over Liffey waters
Dublin's bridges

Opening on the 20 May 2014, the Rosie Hackett Bridge is the newest of twenty-one bridges that cross over the River Liffey. The Liffey runs through the heart of Dublin, dividing the city into North and South. The Rosie Hackett Bridge is the only bridge named after a woman, although Island Bridge was originally known as Sarah Bridge after Sarah Fane (1764–1793), wife of John Fane (1759–1841), Earl of Westmorland

and appointed Lord Lieutenant of Ireland in 1789. Sarah Fane laid the foundation stone for the bridge which was named in her honour. When the Irish Free State was formed in 1922, many of the bridges were renamed as the government of the day broke away from connections to the British Empire.

The twenty-one bridges that now cross the River Liffey from Chapelizod to the sea are:

Anna Livia Bridge (1753)
Island Bridge (1792)
Liffey Viaduct (1877)
Seán Heuston Bridge (1828)
Seán Sherwin Bridge (1982)
Rory O'Moore Bridge (1861)
Mellows Bridge (1768)
James Joyce Bridge (2003)
Father Mathew Bridge (1818)
O'Donovan Rossa Bridge (1816)
Grattan Bridge (1875)
Millennium Bridge (1999)
Ha'penny Bridge (1816)
O'Connell Bridge (1877)
Rosie Hackett (2014)
Butt Bridge (rebuilt 1932)
Loopline Bridge (1891)
Matt Talbot Bridge (1978)

O'Donovan Rossa Bridge

Seán O'Casey Bridge (2005)
Samuel Beckett Bridge (2009)
East Link Bridge (1984)

For many Irish people, O'Connell Bridge represents the heart of their capital city; it crosses the River Liffey at the centre of the city carrying pedestrians, buses, trams and cars across its vast expanse. Unusually for a traffic bridge, O'Connell Bridge is five metres (16.4 feet) wider than it is long. In an elaborate hoax two brothers placed a commemorative bronze plaque on O'Connell Bridge dedicated to the fictitious Father Pat Noise who apparently

The Ha'penny Bridge

drowned after plunging into the River Liffey in 1919. The plaque remained unnoticed for two years until a journalist started to question its provenance and the truth was revealed. Dublin Council wanted to remove it but the story captured the public imagination and the plaque remained.

Opened weeks before the dawning of the new millennium, the Millennium Bridge was the second pedestrian-only bridge across the River Liffey. Prior to that, the Ha'penny Bridge was the only pedestrian-only bridge. Although officially known as the Liffey Bridge since 1922, Dublin's most iconic bridge has been called the Wellington Bridge, the Metal

Bridge, and the Triangle or Iron Bridge. It is most commonly known as the Ha'penny Bridge because pedestrians infamously had to pay a ha'penny toll to cross it. When the bridge opened in May 1816 William Walsh purchased the lucrative lease which collected a ha'penny from pedestrians at the turnstiles either side. The turnstiles were removed in 1919 and the lease was dropped. When the bridge first opened in 1816, 450 people crossed the bridge daily. Now approximately 30,000 trips are made across the bridge each day. Named after the playwright, the Seán O'Casey Bridge is the final pedestrianized bridge in Dublin.

THE CHIME IN THE SLIME
Costing £250,00 in 1996, a digital clock weighing almost 1,000 kg (2204.62lbs) with a solid steel frame measuring 12 metres (39.3 feet) long, 1.9 metres (6.2 feet) deep by 7.8 metres (25.5 feet) wide was placed in the River Liffey on the western side of O'Connell Bridge. Switched

on to great fanfare on the evening of 15 March 1996, the idea was that the illuminated clock would count down the seconds to the 21st century. Passers-by could purchase postcards printed on the spot telling them exactly how many seconds there were to the year 2000. From the outset the Millennium Clock was beset with problems; it was not as waterproof as it should have been and consistently showed the wrong time, it became covered in an unidentifiable green slime which when coupled with the murky nature of the River Liffey rendered the clock unreadable. Locals soon gave it the moniker the **Chime in the Slime.** *Nine months after it was switched on it was unceremoniously fished from the river — three years before the millennium celebrations.*

Cork

From feen to Ford
Cork and the Model T Ford

Henry Ford was born in Dearborn, Michigan in the USA on 30 July 1863, the son of Irish emigrant William Ford (1826–1905). William Ford was born in Ballinascarthy, County Cork. He left Ireland for Quebec in 1847 at the height of the Great Famine following his family's eviction from their tenant farm. His mother did not survive the long voyage. Other members of Ford's family had left Cork in the 1830s, settling in Dearborn, Michigan. William joined them here and settled into farming. He married the adopted daughter of a fellow Cork man, Mary Litogot Ahern. Henry Ford was their first son but unfortunately Mary died during childbirth in 1876. Three years later a sixteen year old Henry left Dearborn and headed for the city. By 1896 Henry had built his first car, and in 1903 he founded the Ford Motor Company.

In the summer of 1912 Henry Ford sailed to Europe for the first time with his wife, Clara, and son Edsel. He visited the place where his ancestors had lived and his father was born. Rumour has it that while in Ballinascarthy Henry attempted to buy his old Ford homestead to transport it back to America to incorporate into his family home. Wily locals decided to increase the price in an attempt to make money from the well-heeled American. Ford soon saw through them and refused to pay the extortionate sum, leaving the Corkmen without a sale.

Despite this, following the trip Henry Ford wrote to the head of the Ford organization in Britain, suggesting that Cork could provide a suitable location for a new Ford manufacturing centre. In 1917 Ford received permission from the

Model T Ford

British Government to build the first Ford plant outside of America at the Marina in Cork. Two years later, the Cork plant produced its first tractor. The plant would later start producing the famous Model T car. The site in Cork remained an important manufacturing facility for the Ford Corporation, employing hundreds of people until a succession of losses forced the Ford Corporation to close the plant in 1984.

Nelson Mandela

We all stand together!
How striking Irish workers helped the fight against apartheid

On 19 July 1984, Mary Manning, a cashier in Dunnes Stores, Henry Street in Dublin, refused to check out a customer's South African grapefruit. She then informed her supervisor that as instructed by her Trade Union, Irish Distributive Administrative Trade Union (IDATU), she would not be handling any produce from South Africa. Manning was immediately suspended. Nine of her colleagues, including shop steward Karen Gearon and a worker from another shop, went on strike in support of the young cashier and what she was standing up for.

At first the strikers were derided by some members of the public but as awareness grew of the situation in South Africa many people joined the workers on the picket line including poet Seamus Heaney and actor Mick Lally. Bishop Desmond Tutu raised the profile of the dispute further when on his way to collect the Nobel Peace Prize in 1984, he asked to meet the strikers. The strike came to an end two years and nine months after it had begun when the Irish government prohibited the importation of South African goods until the apartheid movement was overthrown. Following his release, Neslon Mandela travelled to Ireland and met with some of workers who had stood up against apartheid in one of the longest ever trade union disputes. Mary Manning has had a street in Johannesburg named after her and in 2015 a plaque was unveiled on Henry Street to commemorate all those who went on strike.

Between the jigs and the reels
The Riverdance phenomenon

Watched by approximately 300 million viewers, the first performance of Riverdance was as an interval act at the 1994 Eurovision Song Contest in Ireland. Riverdance is now a cultural phenomenon that has toured the globe, watched by millions of people in cities as far apart as London, New York, and Tokyo.

Back in the twentieth century, Ireland used to do well at the Eurovision Song Contest and following Niamh Kavangh's win in 1993 with the song *In Your Eyes* Ireland was set to host the following years' contest. Inspired by an earlier piece he had conceived for the 1984 Eurovision interval act Timepiece, Bill Whelan composed the breathtaking score for Riverdance. Add the choreography of Jean Butler and Michael Flatley, two Irish-American formally trained Irish dancers, and the piece was elevated. It was a mix of traditional and contemporary both in terms of music and dance. Flatley and Butler were the lead dancers and the climax of the piece involved twenty-four dancers joining the enigmatic Flatley and Butler onstage as the music reached a powerful crescendo. The effect was mesmerising and the audience were on their feet. Ireland went on to win the Eurovision with a song by Paul Harrington and Charlie McGettigan called *The Rock 'n' Roll kids*. Riverdance went on to become a full theatre show making worldwide stars of Jean Butler and Michael Flatley. It is the most successful Irish stage show of all time and continues to tour the world over twenty years later.

INDEX

Amazing and Extraordinary
Facts: Scotland
Douglas Skelton
ISBN: 978-1-910821-14-5

Amazing and Extraordinary
Facts: London
Stephen Halliday
ISBN: 978-1-910821-02-2

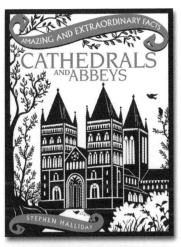

Amazing and Extraordinary
Facts: Cathedrals and Abbeys
Stephen Halliday
ISBN: 978-1-910821-04-6

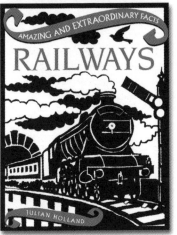

Amazing and Extraordinary
Facts: Railways
Julian Holland
ISBN: 978-1-910821-00-8

For more great books visit our website at **www.rydonpublishing.co.uk**

THE AUTHOR

Sarah Elliott holds a degree in Modern History and recently obtained an MA in Irish History from Maynooth University. She is interested in all facets of Irish life and has published books on subjects as diverse as the Irish beard and GAA. Sarah works in the Irish book trade and lives in North County Dublin.

ACKNOWLEDGEMENTS

A big thank you to my family particularly my Mam for casting her eye over the text and Dara, Hazel, Kieran, Konni and Dad for their helpful advice and suggestions while I was compiling facts: you are amazing and extraordinary people! And thanks to all at Rydon, particularly my editor Verity.

PICTURE CREDITS